Prayer, Fear
and our Powers

Also by Flora Wuellner

Prayer, Fear and our Inner Wounds

Prayer, Fear and our Powers

Finding our healing, release and growth in Christ

FLORA WUELLNER

eagle

Guildford, Surrey

British Library Cataloguing in Publication Data. A catalogue record for this book is available from the British Library.

Originally published in the US by The Upper Room, Nashville, Tennessee. This edition Published in 1998 in the UK by Eagle, an imprint of Inter Publishing Service (IPS) Ltd, St Nicholas House, 14 The Mount, Guildford, Surrey GU2 5HN.

Scripture quotations not otherwise identified are from the Revised Standard Version of the Bible, © 1946, 1952, 1971 by the Division of Christian Education of the National Council of the Churches of Christ in the USA, and are used by permission.

Any scripture quotations designated AP is the author's paraphrase.

Appendix 1 and Appendix 2 were originally published in *Prayer and Our Bodies* by Flora Wuellner (Nashville, The Upper Room), copyright © 1987 Flora Wuellner.

Typeset by Eagle Publishing, Guildford
Printed by
ISBN No: 0 86347

This book is dedicated with delight to our grandchildren, Paul, Luke, and Flora Zsofia, as they explore and celebrate their new growing powers.

Contents

Introduction

As God's love deepens our inner healing, our inner gifts rise with power. This book, started in Advent and finished in the season of Pentecost, is based upon the supreme gift of God to our world, the gift of Jesus. Through the incarnate, risen Christ, we see and experience the limitless love of God. Somewhere I have read beautiful words: "Christmas is the look of love in God's eyes." But during *every* great season of the church year and during each season of our own lives, we are invited to enter into the healed, released empowerment of God's children.

Often we fear the implications of God's love for us. Many of us fear the promised gifts and powers: the misuse of them, the mystery of them, the new risks and pain we will experience, the new responsibilities of freedom. It is frightening as well as exhilarating to know that as we awaken and are healed, our God-given powers and gifts begin to come forth with fullness.

This book is written to help us (beginning with me) to hear God's invitation to face and heal the fear of our powers, to claim our gifts, to embrace the new joy and the new pain.

This book can be read slowly, meditatively; or, it can be read quickly through, returning later to practice the suggested meditations. The meditations at the close of each

chapter are offered to you, the reader, in a spirit of
freedom and respect for your own timing and your own
unique relationship with God. I hope you will claim the
right to change the suggested symbolism or imagery in
any way that is right for you. You may find some meditations do not help you at this time. You may find that
others meet your needs, but with some changes of order
and wording. You may wish to return to some meditations several times. You might decide to tape your own
voice reading them aloud or, even better, to write your
own meditations in your own words.

Some readers may wish to experience some of the
meditations only in the setting of a small, trusted group,
at least at first. Anyone leading or guiding in groups
should always be sensitive to and respectful of the freedom, choice, and timing of group members. Don't assume that group members will claim their inner
freedoms. Explicit permission should *always* be given
before each guided meditation to change inwardly the
symbolism and the wording, to stop at any point, or to
withdraw entirely from any meditation.

Prayerful meditations are offered to supplement, not to
replace, any needed medical or psychological therapy.
One of the greatest sources of inner healing is the loving
fellowship, nurture, and strength of the Church, the
Body of Christ. I urge all readers to find a loving church
family.

May God bless and guide you in the reading of this
book and in the adventure of your growing.

1

God's Loving Call
To Our Empowerment

"They who wait for the Lord . . . shall mount up with wings like eagles," our pastor read from Isaiah 40:31 one autumn Sunday morning. As a small, bored child fidgeting in the pew, those words caught my surprised attention. Just the day before, my parents had called me outdoors to watch the wild geese, soaring in V-formation, flying south. They filled the air with the sound of beating wings and exultant cries. Every fall and spring it was a shared family thrill to watch the wild, free, yet disciplined power of these geese flying over Michigan.

Now, as our pastor read about God calling forth our strength like that of soaring eagles, I remembered the exultation of the flying geese.

So, God likes that kind of thing, I mused. How had I got it into my head that God preferred things to be very quiet, subdued, and resigned?

Then something even more surprising rose within me. *The Bible is saying that God wants me to be like that!* I thought this over. I felt excited. I also felt a little afraid.

Twenty years later, a young mother, I stood at the door of my baby daughter's room. She was sitting up for the very first time, holding the crib bars with one hand. Her back was toward the door, so I could not see her face; but I could see her delight in her new empowerment in every muscle of that little back.

This was another vivid, symbolic moment for me. As I felt that wave of joyful pride at sharing in *her* joy in her new power, I remembered again the awed delight I felt as I watched the wild geese in their released power. *Does God feel this way?* I wondered. *Does God feel this way, only immeasurably more so, when sharing our births, our rebirths, our awakenings, our risings up, our responses, our giftedness, our growing empowerment?*

How, indeed, have we got it fixed into our heads that God wants us, made in the divine image of God's own self, to be passive, resigned, colorless, powerless? Why have we so misunderstood the nature of God's love that we thought God was jealous or angry at our gifts and powers and our longing to express them? Why have we had a deep fear that God might punish us or cut us down to size the minute we began to rejoice in our strengths?

We see nothing of anger or jealousy in Jesus as he came into the villages and walked among the people (men and women as ordinary as you and me), inviting and challenging fishermen, housewives, tax collectors, farmers, rich people, poor people, priests, and women drawing water out of wells to enter into their full powers as God's people.

We see him sending his friends, his disciples, into the villages and cities, giving them the power to love and heal, to call forth, to rebuke evil. We see him giving the power of sight to the blind and the gift of walking and running to the lame. Never once did he tell a disabled person that tragedy was God's will for him or her. We see him calling forth the dignity and strength of each person he encountered.

We see Jesus, the night before his death, telling his close friends that he never wanted them to think of themselves as his servants. He wanted them as *friends*. Servants obey orders because they have to, but friends reveal their hearts to each other and serve each other freely (John 15:15).

We, the friends of Jesus, are not to think of ourselves as servants, as instruments lying inertly in God's hands or as mere functional channels to be used like electric wires. We are invited to that ecstatic, creative union that God longed for in the beginning—when the human being was made in God's own likeness and God walked with us as daily companion and lover.

There is nothing in the world more exciting than seeing and sharing in the healing, release, and empowerment of another human being. A few days ago I talked with a young woman who has been near death many times. For years she has been desperately ill in body and even more wounded in relationships. Now we sat in her sunlit room, looking out into the heart of a great pine tree. She shared with me the story of her long, slow adventure into healing and her deepening joy in God.

"I remember so well what it feels like to be so sick and depressed that I could not walk a block to buy my own groceries," she told me. "Now I'm beginning to feel like Lazarus rising out of the tomb. I don't know where this new strength will lead me. All I know is that I've never felt so alive. And the best thing about it is that I feel God is so *happy* about me. This is the way God wanted me to feel all along."

As I listened to her story, I thought of a middle-aged man I knew and the deep bitterness he had felt over his broken marriage. To his surprise, as his inner hurt was healed he felt an incredible energy and power rising in him. He wanted to *sing* for the first time in his life. He wanted to sing, powerfully, passionately. "I feel as though something that was strangling my heart and throat has finally let go. Now I can take a deep breath and sing," he exclaimed.

He is no opera star. He knows that and doesn't care. But as he opens his mouth and sings in choirs and community groups, he feels the joyous power of God flowing into and through him.

13

I have never known an exception. As we allow God's healing to come deeply into our lives, healing us of our inner wounds, new, almost unbelievable powers rise passionately within us.

The new powers do not always manifest themselves through what we *do*. We are also released to new ways of *being*. We have heard that delightful story in Luke 10:38-42 in which Jesus' friends Mary and Martha, each in her own way, were trying to welcome him into their home. Mary released herself from the anxious, compulsive cooking and serving (in spite of Martha's protests) in order to sit quietly with Jesus, listening and sharing as a friend. This was an almost incredibly bold and empowered choice for a woman in that time and culture. It is still a bold and empowered choice in our time and culture for any of us to let God release us from our compulsive lifestyles, to claim spaces, rest, healthy boundaries, and times of Sabbath in our daily lives.

Whatever our traps, our inner prisons, our hopelessness, our gray, rigid lifestyles, our resigned, mediocre expectations, God longs to free us. God longs for us to rise with fully spread, powerful wings, no longer helpless, cringing children, but renewed and bold, close to God's heart.

The summer I was twenty-one, I was leaving home for my first job two thousand miles away, in a western state where we had no friends. I think back to my mother and how she must have felt as she helped me choose my suitcases and buy my ticket. I think, with awed gratitude, how she did *not* offer to drive me there and to help me get settled. I remember her expression when she learned there was no doctor or railroad or airport nearer than fifty miles from where I was to be located. I saw her expression, but I also saw how she refrained from protest. "Spread your beautiful wings, darling," were her releasing words as I boarded the train.

I have carried those empowering words of release in

my heart ever since, especially when facing new adventure and feeling timidity and old habit holding me down. It is God's voice.

During Advent, Christmas, and Easter, we hear a lot about the angels. Whether we think of them as symbols or realities, they are shown in scripture and song and art as the powerful messengers of God's love. In ancient paintings they are portrayed with two vast wings by which they swiftly and gloriously bring the news of God's desire for us. But in the sixth chapter of Isaiah, I read an almost overwhelming description of the seraphim, the angels closest to God:

> Each had six wings: with two he covered his face, and with two he covered his feet, and with two he flew. And one called to another and said: "Holy, holy, holy is the Lord of hosts; the whole earth is full of his glory." And the foundations of the thresholds shook at the voice of him who called.
>
> —Isaiah 6:2-4

Does this sound as if God were jealous of the power, beauty, and strength of that messenger? This angelic being, the one closest to God, has been given not only two wings, but *six* wings! This angelic being has an exultant voice which shakes the foundations like an earthquake. I see this ancient story as a witness that the closer we come to God, the more profound, distinct, and passionately alive we become, able to receive and express every empowered gift God gives us. I see this as a witness that it is God's own longing and intention that we become as like unto God's own creative, loving heart as possible.

Was this the radiant vision shared with Jesus when he went alone into the wilderness after the overwhelming empowerment he experienced during his baptism? In that long, lonely inner struggle we call his temptation, he was given grave choices to make about those immense powers he had been given. When he finally made the choice to renounce manipulative, coercive shortcuts and to work within God's mystery and love, he returned to his hometown and shared his vision.

He stood up before those in the synagogue at Nazareth and read from the book of Isaiah (that same book which shows us the six-winged angels and tells us that in God we will fly like eagles):

> The Spirit of the Lord is upon me, because he has anointed me to preach good news to the poor. He has sent me to proclaim release to the captives and recovering of sight to the blind, to set at liberty those who are oppressed, to proclaim the acceptable year of the Lord.
>
> —Luke 4:18-19

I believe that this was spoken, not only two thousand years ago in Nazareth, but also now, this moment, in our lives and in our hearts. God, through Christ, comes to the poverty of our inner and outer lives; comes to our sightlessness; comes into our traps, our prisons, into whatever binds and blinds us, and speaks the word of release and empowerment.

That "acceptable year of the Lord" which Jesus joyously proclaimed referred to that special year of Jubilee in ancient Israel, in which all debts were released, sins forgiven, and slaves and prisoners were set free throughout the land. I believe that Jesus was telling them then, and us now, that this is no longer a release to be expected only every fifty years. It is now. It is forever. It can become true for us in the midst of whatever life we are living. For this is now the country of God's own heart, and this is the way things are in that heart which holds us and loves us.

What can this mean for each of us now? Let us test these waters by letting God's heart speak personally and directly to each of us.

Suggested Meditation

As you sit or lie down in a relaxed position, take a few deep, but gentle breaths. Think of God's loving and eager strength around you, holding you firmly and safely.

As you slowly read these biblical verses of invitation, let each one speak to you as if you were hearing it for the first time. If one of them especially touches you deeply, just stay with that verse.

Do these verses seem in some special way to relate to your life as it is now? Do you feel excitement? If so, let it expand. Do you feel some anxiety or fear? Don't resist the anxiousness. Accept its presence, knowing that God understands that much pain and woundedness underlies this fear. The healing of fear will come later.

If you have no special feeling at this time, don't push or contrive an appropriate response. It is enough at this point just to let God speak to your heart and to listen.

> The voice of my beloved!
>   Behold he comes,
> leaping upon the mountains,
> . . . .
> Behold, there he stands
>   behind our wall,
> gazing in at the windows,
>   looking through the lattice.
> My beloved speaks and says to me:
> "Arise, my love, my fair one,
>   and come away;
> . . . .
>   the time of singing has come."
> —The Song of Solomon 2:8-12

They who wait for the Lord
  shall renew their strength,
  they shall mount up with wings like eagles,

they shall run and not be weary,
they shall walk and not faint.

—Isaiah 40:31

Behold, I am doing a new thing;
now it springs forth, do you not perceive it?
—Isaiah 43:19

Awake, O sleeper, and arise from the dead,
and Christ shall give you light.
—Ephesians 5:14

I came that they might have life, and have it abundantly.
—John 10:10

You are the light of the world. A city set on a hill cannot be hid.

—Matthew 5:14

I am the vine, you are the branches. Abide in me, and I in you. As the branch cannot bear fruit by itself, unless it abides in the vine, neither can you, unless you abide in me.

—John 15:5,4

May you be strengthened with all power, according to his glorious might . . . giving thanks to the Father, who has qualified us to share in the inheritance of the saints in light.

—Colossians 1:11,12

As you reflect on all, or just one or two, of these verses, ask God to show you where in your life you need light, healing, release, new empowerment. Don't try to do anything about this now. Just gently note what you seem to sense.

Let your attention move through your body and note

any bodily areas which seem to be contracted in anxiety or defense. Don't try to change this forcibly. Sense that God's tenderness lays hands on these bodily areas and that warmth begins to flow into them.

When ready, bring your meditation to a gentle close.

2

Healing a Central Fear Of Empowerment

Most of us feel at least some fear of our empowerment. Perhaps as you read and reflected on the words of God's invitation in the preceding chapter, you felt some anxiety, some shrinking.

Why is anxiety so deeply intermingled with our longing? Is it the awesome mystery of the greatness buried deeply within us? Is it the fear of being out of control, overwhelmed by inner forces? Is it the likelihood of risk-taking, of new ways of loving and suffering yet to be experienced? Is it the fear of loneliness? It is all of these reasons and more.

One of the deepest fears is the possibility of abuse of empowerment. Each of us has, at some point in our lives, experienced this abuse. Sometimes we have been the abuser, exerting manipulative force over others. At the time, probably we thought we were acting for the good of the other. But as we look back, we are appalled at the harm we did.

Or, perhaps we bitterly remember how it felt when we ourselves were powerless and others controlled and manipulated us. It is hard to be healed of the sense of helplessness, anger, and fear.

I remember one evening in a college dormitory, over thirty years ago. It did not seem, at the time, a very serious incident compared with the worldwide, unspeakable abuses of power we read about every day. But looking back on it, it seems a microcosm, a little psychodrama, similar on a small scale to what can happen on a large scale.

A group of young women were talking and sharing experiences one evening, curled up comfortably in one of the bedrooms. We had often shared each other's thoughts this way before, but that evening something new and ominous began to happen. Patricia, a girl of powerful, emotional influence over others, began to question and probe deeply into some secret she was convinced Margaret was hiding. For over an hour she probed, needled, and cross-examined until Margaret broke into convulsive sobbing and poured out many family secrets she had not freely chosen to share, all dignity shattered.

Patricia sat quietly watching her. There was a satisfied gleam in her eyes. The rest of us sat there, submitting to what was going on, feeling ashamed and faintly unclean. And Margaret? She had the look on her face of one who had been violated.

We have seen, experienced, or perpetrated similar incidents in our families, in our schools, in our work places. We have seen it happening in certain types of churches, prayer or therapy groups. Through the experience of such assaults (often going on in the name of spiritual guidance), we have learned to distrust power. Can *any* power, especially our own, ever be really trusted? Is the old saying true that all power corrupts, and absolute power corrupts absolutely? Is the word *power* synonymous with demonic forces by very definition? Should Christians renounce power within themselves?

We look deeper in our hearts. Do we really trust even God's power? Won't God punish us, after all, if we grow too tall? Even if we are reminded that the angels closest to God are the most free, the most powerful, can we really believe that this will be true for us? Will God invade us, force us, crush our dignity as Patricia did Margaret? Is this deep fear of an invading God the heart of the reason that so many of us avoid a deeper relationship with God?

On the table in my counseling room I have a beautiful little bronzed statue of the hands of God, tenderly holding a trusting child. The hands are bigger than the child's whole body. I love that statue and often look at it when I am counseling, praying, or just relaxing. But recently, while talking with a woman who had undergone brutal punishment and abuse as a little child, I suddenly thought that it must hurt her to look at that statue on my table. She had been a small, trusting child, and the large hands of those people around her had beaten and punished her repeatedly. Her trust was abused at its very heart.

The symbol of the hands of God is my favorite symbol of God's loving strength. But what does such a symbol do to a person who has known abuse? How can such a person learn to trust God or any symbol of God and God's power?

We who are in spiritual leadership have not yet taken seriously enough the terror of both power and powerlessness which so many people feel. Perhaps we leaders have not always looked with honesty at our own deep inner fears. Our defenses, masks, and walls have grown around most of us during years of powerlessness and woundedness. These defenses, many of us felt, kept us at least somewhat defended, held us up, kept us moving when nothing else seemed to help. These masks seemed to provide so many of us (at least for a while) with some kind of dignity, privacy, identity. We have held on to them because we felt we needed them so desperately.

Then along come spiritual leaders who tell us to "take a leap of faith," or who tell us to "let go and let God," or who ask us to surrender all that we are to God all at one time. This is completely insensitive to the fact that the

very *thought* of letting go to anyone (especially to someone who claims limitless power) stirs up our deepest
hurts and fears. What frightening, humiliating thing will
happen to us if we do let ourselves surrender to those
enormous hands? What cruel rocks will we be allowed to
fall upon if we do take that leap of faith?

It is time that our spiritual approach—our spiritual
language in counseling, guidance, retreats, hymns,
prayers, sermons—catches up with what any therapist
knows: large numbers of us are wounded in the very
heart of trust, frightened of God's power.

Some months ago I talked with a man who had been an
active, devoted member of a strict religious community.
He and his family had entered this group in good faith,
eager for spiritual companionship, guidance, and
growth. At first it was an inspiring and empowering
commitment. But, as the years went on, the gifted leader
became increasingly egocentric in his need to dominate
and control. The freedom and identities of the group
members began to be crushed.

"I saw I had to leave the group before it was too late,"
he told me. "I left and my family came with me. Outwardly I am free, but inwardly I still feel that shock and
anger. And what's worse, all this was done to me in the
name of Jesus. How can I trust even *Jesus* any more?"

A long time of healing was needed before he began to
realize and then to trust that it was not Jesus, it was not
God, who was responsible for the crushing manipulation
he had undergone. All through Christian history there
have been and (God help us!) still are things done in the
name of Jesus which are utterly hideous and repellant to
the true spirit of Jesus!

"Not every one who says to me, 'Lord, Lord,' shall
enter the kingdom of heaven, but he who does the will of
my Father who is in heaven" (Matt. 7:21).

And what *is* the will of God in heaven? The will of God
can be translated as the passionate longing of God. We

24

can be sure of this: whatever crushes us or other human beings, whatever denies our free choices, whoever shows contempt for the dignity of others is totally violating God's will.

Is this what Jesus was facing there alone in the wilderness? As he strove to understand the full meaning of the empowered gifts God had given him, was his main temptation to turn those almost limitless powers into manipulation? Was he tempted to manipulate nature by turning the stones into bread? It would seem so. He was tempted to manipulate other people by forcing the kingdoms of the world under his authority. Apparently he was even tempted to manipulate God by throwing himself off of a high place to prove that God would catch him in midair. But then, and for the rest of his life, he refused to depersonalize those whom he encountered by manipulating them.

His passionate mission was to release people from bondage of all kinds. He loved others with the love that does not imprison, but liberates.

Here we see in fullness the God of infinite power who has forever renounced the use of force. God's loving power is not the same as force. And our love is not submission.

The Creator we see through Jesus honors, heals, celebrates, and empowers our very being, our identity. God says this moment in our central heart: "I love your freedom more than you do. I am the one who releases you from bondage of every kind. I even permit you to say no to me. Even when you try to escape from your identity, from your empowered freedom, I will forever return them to you. When you hear my call of love and when you share with me your fears, hurts, and longings, I will heal you. I will call you into marriage with me; I will endow you with gifts and call forth your deep hidden powers which I gave you before birth."

But our healing and trust grow slowly for most of us.

25

And when they do start to grow, it is so tempting to hurry the process. Longing for the full experience of life with God, our temptation is to push open inner doors in a hurry, to knock down the defensive walls, to tear off those masks that for so long have hidden our real selves. It is tempting to do this not only to ourselves, but also to those others we are helping.

Do not permit this to be done to you or to anyone else. It can be dangerous to remove forcibly the defenses which held us in one piece for so long. These walls and doors are living tissue, the very presence of our hurt and need. Our tears and pain and fear take the shape of walls and closed doors and masks. God lovingly encounters these defenses, knowing them for what they are—our own wounded hearts.

And we begin to experience the awesome truth: the more deeply we let God move into our hearts then the more we experience God's power, the more our own power is released by God, and the *less* we wish or need to use force on ourselves or on anyone else. The radical change has begun within us. The word *radical* refers to *root*. The divine healing love moves to the very root, the deepest, center part of ourselves.

Our defensive walls will be healed into our healthy borders. Our inwardly closed doors will, slowly or swiftly, become open portals to new and richer gifts of God and others. The very judgmental, rigid, dictatorial defenses within us (so long used for resistance or force) will themselves be transformed into the giftedness of passionate compassion.

Suggested Meditation

This is God's word to the wounded, the frightened, the defensive:

> Then you shall see and be radiant,

your heart shall thrill and rejoice;
because the abundance of the sea
shall be turned to you
. . . .
Whereas you have been forsaken and hated,
with no one passing through,
I will make you majestic for ever,
a joy from age to age.
. . . .
I will make your overseers peace
and your taskmasters righteousness.
Violence shall no more be heard in your land,
devastation or destruction within your borders;
you shall call your walls Salvation,
and your gates Praise.
. . . .
Your sun shall no more go down,
nor your moon withdraw itself;
for the Lord will be your everlasting light,
and your days of mourning shall be ended.
. . . .
I am the Lord;
in its time I will hasten it.
—Isaiah 60: 5, 15, 17-18, 20, 22

Sit or lie down in a comfortable, relaxed position. Breathe slowly, deeply, but gently. Think of God's love, the Healer, close to you in whatever form, inner symbolic picture, or feeling is best for you. The Healer may come to you in the inner picturing of Jesus, in the sense of light or warmth around your body, or in the thought of comforting words. Or even in some other way. Rest for a while in God's closeness.

Remember that at any point you may change the wording of this prayerful meditation. At any point you may leave this meditation and move into some other form of prayer. If you sense that God is bringing you into light sleep, that is fine.

But if ready, ask yourself, in God's presence, how you

really feel about God. Is there some fear, some anxiety or distrust? Do not try to force any inner surrender. Just let your anxiousness be there, perhaps in the form of a frightened little child. Can you picture or sense in what way the Healer shows tenderness towards that inner frightened child?

Think of some memory, recent or long past, when your trust was abused by the power of another person. If you feel anger, don't try to hurry past that anger. Let it be there with you and the Healer, maybe in symbolic form. Your anger will not shock or frighten God.

Where in your body do you feel the old anger or anxiousness? Does it feel focused in your heart area? Or do you feel it focused in your jaw, behind your eyes, in your back, in your abdomen or hands or feet? Does that area feel numb and cold? Does it feel hot and burning? Does it feel tightly contracted in the muscles?

Picture or sense the Healer gently laying warm healing hands on that bodily part. Of, if the thought of touch seems intrusive or threatening, just let warm light flow into that bodily area. Lay your own hands on that part of your body if you can do this comfortably.

Rest quietly, letting your body signal to you the anger, the wound, the anxiety you feel. Your body is your lifelong, loving companion and truth-teller. If you feel no special fear or anger, but just numbness, don't force an "appropriate" emotion. Just rest in the presence of God's warm, healing light.

You are in a safe place. Pehaps you can inwardly picture the Healer lifting each feeling or memory you have, cradling or embracing it like a child. If you do not feel comfortable with this inner picture, let God suggest comfort and tenderness in some other way.

When ready, come slowly out of your meditation. Feel the floor or the chair beneath your body holding you, the earth beneath that chair or floor holding you. Breathe gently and slowly and deeply. You may wish to massage your face and hands lightly and gently. Give loving thanks to God in whatever way is right for you, and close the meditation.

3

Encountering the Mystery Of Our Powers

I talked recently with a wise friend, reflecting together on why we are so often afraid of our potential powers and gifts. "I think we fear the awesome *mystery* of our inner powers," she said thoughtfully. "What will we become? What will we turn into?"

She is right, of course. We fear the area of our empowerment not only because we have experienced the abuse of powers, but also because of the almost instinctive shiver we feel at the thought of limitless growing, deepening, expanding. What will we be like? Will we be recognizable? What will be asked or expected of us? What unpredictable responsibilities will come our way? Will we be lonely, set apart from other people? Will we move and live beyond the abilities of our parents, our spouses, our best friends, our spiritual leaders? Will we have to give up all our excuses, all forms of dependence? A student once expressed this fear in an unforgettable remark: "Do I want to be powerless with others or to be empowered alone?"

Some years ago I visited a grove of redwood trees on the California coast. I brought back with me a tiny pot containing earth and redwood seeds, along with the instructions for their planting and raising. As I watered the earth in the little pot and put it on a window sill, I thought of the fantastic contrast between the tiny green blade which would soon appear and the gigantic, full-grown redwood tree (which it might become some day) more than 300 feet high. Some of these trees may have flourished when Jesus was born in Bethlehem.

And then I thought of John's reflection: "Beloved, we are God's children now; it does not yet appear what we shall be, but we know that when he appears we shall be like him, for we shall see him as he is" (1 John 3:2).

What immensities and depths will be revealed in us as we increasingly enter into not only the love of God, but also the indescribable mystery of God?

Already we know, even on this earth, that we use only a tiny percent of the total capacity of our brains. Already we have experienced our amazing capacity for creative work, for clear, efficient thinking in an emergency situation. What sorts of giants are sleeping within us? What mysterious powers lurk there? What will happen if they get out?

We feel this fear with special poignancy if we are not yet in touch with or aware of a strong, central identity within us that can set reasonable day-by-day goals for our selves and maintain healthy boundaries as we grow and relate to others. Is it this lack of awareness of the inner guiding power that makes us so afraid that we will go, and grow, out of control once we start growing?

Is it possible that this underlies the deep fear the anorexic person feels when the weight begins to go on? Could this be the underlying fear of the person who is compulsively tidy and overcontrolled at the first sign of disorder or dissent? Might this underlie the fears many of us have of intimacy and spontaneity and the difficulty in expressing anger, grief, love, praise? Is this why it is so hard to make decisions, take action, set limits, assert ourselves?

Perhaps we think that our inner powers will get so out of control that there "won't be any *me* any more!" Or maybe we feel, *If others find out what I'm really feeling, thinking, or want to do, they won't like me anymore.*

Most of us feel these fears and hesitancies at some times in our lives. Unfortunately, there are too many types of family and church structures, and too many forms of spiritual teaching which tremendously increase these fears within us.

I was sickened recently when I visited a home in which the small children were punished painfully and bodily every time they hesitated to obey an order or expressed any anger or cried with disappointment. This family belongs to a church which teaches that we are born evil and therefore a child's will must be "broken" beginning with babyhood. They believe it is not enough to *guide* a child's will with loving firmness; rather, they must *break* it. Therefore, a baby's head is forcibly held down until the child consents to nap; a little child is whipped with a switch when it shows anger. These rigid rules stop just short of child abuse that could be reported legally. But they are severe and consistent enough to teach a child to distrust any spontaneous feelings of anger, grief, or dissent. Since these punishments are continued in this community up through the teenage years, the growing person feels deeply evil at his or her emotional core and believes that God watches each feeling and action as a judgmental punisher. Under this training, it becomes almost impossible to be honest about one's real needs and longings. Perhaps what we fear the most (especially when young) is disapproval and exclusion from our close communities. Rather than be cut off from their surrounding relationships, men and women in such a repressive community find it easier and safer to supress any anger, doubt, or rebellion, or to confess these feelings as sinful.

The opposite extreme can be equally frightening. Children brought up without *any* firm guidelines, who are shown no ways by which they can safely encounter and understand their powerful feelings, who are allowed to make life-changing decisions at very young ages, often become anxious about their powers. They fear going out of control and often swing between the two extremes of rigid self-control or living without any limits.

Even when brought up with healthy but gentle guidelines, people still find it difficult in our modern culture to feel a sense of real control over their lives. Faced with the mysteries of love, sexuality, illness, hospitalization, rearing of children, spiritual growth, the educational process, and death, we all need to help each other experience more options, more choices, more healthy control.

Many people, deeply anxious about their inner powers, either overcontrolled or out of limits, will respond to their own mystery with dependency and/or addictions. These are attempts to shortcut the growth process to empowerment or to deaden the fear and pain.

Others will try to separate themselves through inner emotional detachment, often under the name of spiritual discipline. Still others will try to overcontrol their own bodies, other people, or their immediate surroundings.

It is helpful, though painful, to observe in ourselves in what controlling ways, or by what total lack of control, we respond to situations that make us anxious. Some of us at these times refuse to meet deadlines, keep appointments, clean up our houses, or answer letters.

Some of us develop little rituals. I have begun to notice in myself one of the first signs that I am becoming anxious about an experience or feeling that I don't want to face. I start some little ritual of control over my immediate surroundings. For example, I may go early to a classroom or retreat room and start pushing chairs around until they are *just so*. I tell myself that I am trying to make things more comfortable for the group members. Apparently I don't trust the group members enough to let them arrange chairs comfortably for themselves. Occasionally

I am honest enough to admit to myself that I'm feeling a little worried about the session to come.

This is a small, unimportant symptom of an anxious need to feel *controlling*, as opposed to being *in control*. But what if this need grows for some of us into a need to become controlling over every detail of our lives in order to crowd out the mystery? What if we try to become controlling of God? I'm beginning to think that much of the new enthusiasm for magic or occult rituals is based on deep fear of the mystery in and around us, the fear of God's own self, and our attempt to control this mystery.

Was this also an aspect of the fierce conflict with temptation that Jesus felt in the wilderness? Was it, perhaps, not only the temptation to force others into the kingdom of heaven, but also the need to feel control over the awesome powers of God within him?

What can heal our fear of the mystery within? A dream came to me many years ago, a dream rich in symbolism and comforting power. I dreamed I was on a strange planet. I looked around and said (in the time-honored science fiction manner), "Take me to your leader." Walking toward me was a green giant, about as tall as a redwood tree or a skyscraper. Gazing up and *up* at him, I asked him if he was the leader. "No," he said, "I have come to carry you to the leader." I asked him how he would get me there, and he told me he would pick me up and carry me in his hand. Looking in terror at his immense height, I told him hurriedly that there had to be some other way by which I could reach the leader. I was simply *not willing* to be picked up and carried at that height. He smiled and said he would go and inquire if there were some other way.

In the next sequence of the dream, I found myself standing in a spaceship, circling the planet. There was a man of normal height standing at the controls. He turned around, gave me a wonderfully tender smile, and said, "I am the leader." I felt relaxed and comfortable with him,

35

and we talked a while about the spaceship and the planet beneath us. Then he remarked quietly, "Have you realized how high up we really are?" I looked through the window and saw that we were many miles higher than the full height of that giant who had frightened me so. But in this little spaceship with the leader (of my height) at my side, I was not afraid. Everything seemed normal and homelike. I looked again out the window and saw the word *amor* (which means *love*) written on the planet beneath us.

Usually I forget my dreams (until I learned to write them down), but this one remained with me in vivid detail for a long time before I began to understand what it really meant. It was a dream about our powers and our fear of our powers. It was a dream which shows that God and our deep inner self understand and respect our anxiousness and fear and will not force us or hurry us. It was a dream showing me that God will come to us at our own level of need and in the way in which we can best receive God's gifts, which, of course, is what the Incarnation is all about. It showed me that this compassionate God is at the controls of our deep inner self. Within that love which fills our bodies and hearts we will be carried to heights we had not dreamed we could reach. And those powerful heights will seem natural and homelike to us.

As I think about this dream and its rich meanings, I think also about the rainbow. The rainbow is a sign to us that the white light (perhaps more powerful than we can bear at this time), when shining through a prism, becomes the color spectrum. We can relate to certain colors more easily than to others, but the rainbow is still essentially the white light coming to us mercifully. Is this another symbol of the Incarnation, in which God came to us in the tenderness of a human being like ourselves, rather than in the frightening manifestation of an angel or the full effulgence of unshaded light?

This kind of God—who does not overwhelm us, who does not blast us, who leads us tenderly step-by-step to our full powers—is the one who is at the very center of our selves, who is at our controls, who will redeem and heal our fears of our central mystery.

Just recently I thought of another meaning, among the many meanings, of John 21, one of my favorite chapters in the New Testament. The risen Jesus, meeting his disciples by the shores of the lake, has cooked breakfast for them, served them, and warmed them by the bonfire. Then he turns to Peter, who has denied him out of terror three times on that night of betrayal. Healing Peter's memory of shame and guilt and fear, Jesus asks him three times if he, Peter, loves him. The first time Peter says he loves him, Jesus replies: "Feed my lambs." The second time Peter expresses his love, Jesus says: "Tend my sheep." The third time Peter responds with love, Jesus says significantly: "Feed my sheep."

I see here not only the deep, healed bonding between Jesus and Peter, but also a profound parable for all of us as we are increasingly healed and affirmed in God's love. Many biblical commentators say that we should not put too much emphasis upon the differences in the original Greek words for *lambs* and *sheep, tend* and *feed*. Perhaps they are right. But I was pastor for some years in the sheep-grazing areas of Wyoming and Idaho, and I observed the different levels of responsibility in the care of sheep.

"Feed my lambs" can be interpreted as the first and easiest level of responsibility. Lambs are born in the very early spring, often when the snow is still deep on the ground. Sometimes the mother has died in the cold or cannot feed the lambs if more than one is born to her. Then the shepherd brings the newborn lamb to his home for his children to feed from a bottle, to keep warm, to nurture. The children may someday become full-grown shepherds, ready to take on the full responsibility for the whole flock, including the tough, weathered rams. But they are not ready for this yet. So they are given the lambs.

"Tend my sheep" is the level of greater responsibility. An older child or young shepherd-in-training is given the tasks of helping to keep the sheep healthy, counting them, guiding them, keeping them in line, learning how to heal their wounds, helping the ewes in labor. Recently I talked with a young seminary student who had been brought up on a sheep ranch. She remembered the cold nights out in the barn, holding the lantern, getting the soapy water ready as her father delivered the ewe of several lambs in multiple birth. She recalled how her father talked gently and firmly to the laboring ewe as she struggled and how it felt to stand by him, watching, learning, helping in the drama of birth.

"Feed my sheep" refers to the most demanding responsibility of all. The shepherd leads the whole flock to new pasture, richer grasslands, perhaps many miles away from home because sheep eat close to the ground and quickly strip the land of nourishment. Often the new grassland is found up in the hills, and the shepherd may have to guide them through dangerous rocky territory, with ravines and cliffs and natural predators. The shepherd feeding the sheep has to be alert enough to keep the sheep away from edges of cliffs, wise enough to notice what shrubs and foliage may be poisonous, strong enough to fend off hyenas or wolves. This is the task of the full-grown, experienced shepherd only.

I find it reassuring to think that God does not demand of my newly born, still fragile powers the full responsibilities. They will come later as my healing deepens, as well as my understanding of the powers and gifts growing in me.

I think it is also important to know that God does not require that everything within us be fully grown and developed at the same time. It is all right to have some levels of nonempowerment within us, to have un-awakened areas, quiescent areas. It is all right not to have made up our minds fully about everything. It is all right to have undeveloped gray areas in which we do not yet feel clear and assertive and strong.

Are these unpowerful aspects within us similar to the void spoken of in Genesis which has not yet been touched by God's creative hand? Are these inner areas the sleeping giants, the unexpressed potential?

Whatever they are, it is reassuring to remember that God has all eternity to bring us fully to life. As long as we are awakening and growing in *some* areas of our lives, and as long as we are allowing God's love deeper and deeper into our lives, we can trust that in the right time, step-by-step, all our inner powers will someday be awakened.

The following suggested meditation helps us to become aware that God loved us, knew us, and empowered us even before we were born, while we were still growing in our mothers' wombs. That even at this very moment God is affirming our central identity, not in just what we do, but in what we *are*.

This helps heal our fear that our inner powers will somehow get out of bounds and overwhelm us. It also helps heal our fear that our inner self does not exist or that it will be overwhelmed by others or by the mystery which surrounds us.

Suggested Meditation

The Lord came . . . saying,
"Before I formed you in the womb I knew you,
and before you were born I consecrated you."
　　　　　　　　　　　　　　　—Jeremiah 1:4-5

For thou didst form my inward parts,
　　thou didst knit me together in my mother's womb.

I praise thee, for thou art fearful and wonderful.

. . . .

Thou knowest me right well;
   my frame was not hidden from thee,
when I was being made in secret,

. . . .

Thy eyes beheld my unformed substance;
   in thy book were written, every one of them,
the days that were formed for me,

. . . .

How precious to me are thy thoughts, O God!
                              —Psalm 139:13-17

Relax your body and breathe slowly, gently, deeply—
without forcing or straining. Think of God's closeness
like gentle hands holding you, or warm sunlight shining
on you, or in some other way that helps you.

Now picture your unborn self, lying in the womb long
ago, or lying within your deep self right now. You are in a
safe place, resting, curled up.

Picture God's loving hands (which never use force) or
God's warm light gently forming your shape, your body,
your boundaries. You are becoming firm, healthy, distinct.

God's loving voice calls your name and then says, "Let
there be *you*."

Then God gently rubs a warm light or oil onto your
little unborn body and says, "I anoint you with empowered light."

See the light and strength beginning to radiate and
shine from your deep, central self, your core. This is
God's own light, God's own love at your center, forming
your identity, shining and expanding.

Rest quietly, giving thanks that God wants there to be a
you; that God is helping that deep central self grow; that
you are precious to God.

As you gently breathe, think of each breath as God
breathing life into you, into every bodily part.

When ready, gently conclude your meditation.

4

Claiming Our Empowerment Through Christ

Just as Jesus called forth his friend Lazarus from the tomb and told his friends to release him from his constricting winding-sheet, so he calls forth every one of us from our constrictions, our death in life.

Just as he raised the little daughter of Jairus from her death-like sleep and told her family to give her something to eat, thus also he raises up the deep sleeping selves within us and offers the bread of life, the nurture, by which we may feel strengthened.

In the Sermon on the Mount, when Jesus speaks of turning the other cheek, returning good for evil, going the second mile, he was not calling us to a life of weakness and passivity. Rather, he was describing the responses that begin to seem *natural* to us as we enter ever deeper into the bonding, the relationship with the living God. To speak of turning the other cheek is *dangerous* for those who have not yet begun to experience the inner empowerment that God gives to our deep, central selves.

The Sermon on the Mount is not a series of commands given to frightened, unprepared, helpless people to render them victims to predators. He was talking to Israel, the people who had already been told, in the deep understanding of Judaic Law, what it meant to know that

God is in the midst of them, affirming, loving, empowering, at every moment.

It is significant that when he talked to those who had not been grounded and trained by God's covenant, such as the Roman centurion, he does not challenge them to release their swords and defenses. Is it perhaps even *more* significant that when he and his disciples left the upper room where they shared the Passover on the night he was betrayed, he suggested they bring swords for their *own* self-defense (Luke 22:36-38). He did not allow them to fight for him, but he did not forbid them to defend themselves. Perhaps in his compassion he realized that they were in such a state of helpless fear they needed those swords. Whatever the explanation, we sense that Jesus is not trying to turn us into helpless victims, but is calling forth our strength from the deepest possible level. Better the sword than absolute helplessness. But better than the sword is the inner union with the living God, "in your midst, a warrior who gives victory" (Zeph. 3:17).

I am thinking of a woman, a lifelong friend whom I admire. As a girl, raised in a well-meaning but very domineering family, she developed an almost explosive temper. It was the only way she knew how to keep her natural boundaries from trespass. It was the only way she knew to preserve some sense of identity.

As her love for God grew, expanded, and healed her, she was able to release her need of fury. It has been years since I have seen her explode in anger. It is not that she is repressing her feelings. On the contrary, the closer to God she has come, the more human she has become. But now the firmness, strength, and self-defining power within her, risen from her healing closeness to Christ, has taken the place of her defensive anger. Christ's love did not strip her of defenses and protection, leaving her a victim to the control of others. But Christ's love gave her another, transformed way to live with others in strength.

As I watch her changing life, I think of Paul's awed witness: "It is no longer I who live, but Christ who lives in me" (Gal. 2:20).

And yet the paradox of this transforming miracle within us is that never before have we so profoundly felt that we were our own true selves. For the love of God through Christ does not wipe out our sense of self, but wakens the self, espouses it, heals it, brings it to heights we never dreamed possible.

Many of us are troubled that that transformation has not yet taken place fully within us. We know ouselves still in many ways dependent upon our swords, our own defenses. But as I shared my thoughts in chapter two, God understands and works mercifully with our defendedness. The older I grow, the more I feel we should not worry too much about whether we are filled with Christian virtues (which mean strengths) or whether or not we are worthy of belonging to Christ. Rather, let us concentrate on one thing: are we learning to move into closer and closer relationship with the living Christ? Our spiritual lives are not a set of rules and disciplines, but rather a living *relationship*, with all the ups and downs, surprises, unexpectedness, and lopsidedness of any growing relationship. All that really matters is that we "abide in the vine" (John 15:4). All that really matters is that, more and more, "Christ may dwell in your hearts through faith" (Eph. 3:17). And then with awe, we watch what begins to happen in our lives, our habits, our relationships, our powers, our gifts.

The transforming friendship, along with the healed gifts, is an instinctive longing within us. We long to be raised like Jairus' daughter from sleep. We long to be released from constriction, like Lazarus. We long to experience change, love, ecstasy. I am convinced that this frustrated longing underlies many forms of addictions, many forms of co-dependent relationships, many attempted shortcuts to empowerment, ecstasy, release.

Think of something which you feel addicted to, compulsive about. I don't mean actions rising from life's necessities or things we do in freedom and celebration. I mean something which has power over us, something that is essentially joyless and an increasing burden, something we need increasingly, obsessively, even though its rewards keep diminishing. It may be something quite trivial, or something gravely life threatening. But it has dominion over us.

This is an addiction. Perhaps we were originally drawn to it because it seemed to give a sense of release, power, self-confidence, even ecstasy. It seemed to give us freedom at first, but now we are its slave. It seemed to offer new life, but now it constricts our life. We longed for the joy it offered and the sense of power. But every day we grow weaker, more joyless.

It may be a relationship. It may be an eating or drinking pattern. It may be sexual promiscuity. It may be a community increasingly destructive to our feeling of self-worth. But we are addicted to it, and we know that it is an addiction because life and freedom are being crushed out of us and yet we cannot seem to free ourselves.

Is this the meaning of that strange, hard saying of Jesus in Matthew 18:8-9, in which he says if our hand, foot, or eye leads us into darkness and sin it is better to cut them off than to be wholly destroyed? This hard saying puzzled and distressed me for years. It did not sound like the Jesus who *healed* so many blind eyes and crippled limbs! Only recently did I realize he was not talking about destroying something *within* us, but rather releasing us from anybody or anything that has addictive dominion *over* us.

In chapter two, I told the story of the man who had been involved for years in a religious cult, which had begun by offering him the experience of joy and abundant life, but as time went on, increasingly assaulted his freedom and identity. As he reflected on his experience, he said with tears in his eyes: "To leave it and to bring my whole family out *was* like cutting off my hand or taking out my eye. But I had to do it, or we would all have been destroyed."

I have heard the same witness from many who felt drawn by God out of an increasingly loveless, joyless marriage which was destroying their health.

The same experience is shared by those who know they must leave a workplace or profession which seems increasingly to stifle the life and giftedness within. It is painful. It is almost like amputation, but they know they must leave.

And any who have been caught by the physical addiction of drugs, alcohol, or promiscuity know well that the pain of leaving their addiction is only one degree less than the pain of remaining.

It is interesting that Jesus said these hard, realistic words while holding a little child in his arms. He had begun by saying that nothing was worse than abusing the trust of "one of these little ones." Was he talking not only about actual children (although, God knows, that warning cannot be repeated often enough in these days when hideous child abuse seems to be increasing), but also about the child of hope, trust, and new life within each of us? Is he saying here that anything is better than allowing the life within us to be destroyed?

Often in the Bible the hand or foot is used as a symbol of empowerment. And often in scripture the symbol of the eye is used to mean enlightenment. If we have entered into any relationship, into any community, into any form of work or action expecting empowerment and enlightenment, and instead are finding increasing weakness and darkness, I believe God is saying to us through these words of Jesus that anything is better than continuing under that addictive dominion. These are the words of God's release. This is God's sanction to leave that relationship. "If then the light in you is darkness, how great is the darkness!" (Matt. 6:23).

We are to claim and reclaim our deep inner strength

and powers through the one who has, all along, understood our longing for release, relatedness, and ecstasy and who has understood why we moved under other powers in search for them. We are not condemned, but embraced.

When we feel powerless against the other powers which claim dominion over our lives, we do not have to use willpower alone, good intentions alone, New Year's resolutions alone. Just as it is God's love which said, and still says, at our very core, forming and affirming our identity, "Let there be you," so is it Christ who speaks the word of radical healing and empowerment at that very core. It is Christ who goes ahead to prepare a place for us (John 14:2). It is Christ who "fronts" for us, who puts the protective light around us, "who called you out of darkness into his marvellous light" (1 Pet. 2:9).

When we feel powerless, we can in the power of prayer see ourselves not only moving near to Christ, but actually moving *within* that Risen Body of light, within the one who is "far above all rule and authority and power and dominion, and above every name that is named, not only in this age but also in that which is to come . . ." (Eph. 1:21).

Out of this radiant power which speaks within us and wraps around us, rise *our* powers, rejoicing in the abundant life.

The church seasons affirm and rejoice in the healing power of Christ, Emmanuel, God with us, released into our personal and our communal lives like the sun rising in the sky or the yeast expanding in the bread.

Advent: The empowerment of the mystery, the expectancy, the promise of God's passionate compassion coming among us.

Christmas: The new life, the Incarnation, the fullness of God born into humanity and born again in our hearts when we welcome it.

Epiphany: The shining forth, the full revealing of the light of Christ into his community, into the whole world, and into our own lives.

Lent: The power of turning around, repentance, the promise of healing salvation among us. The vision of God's own suffering, weeping in the midst of our own pain, and of God's love receiving our wounds into that divine heart.

Easter: The power of new life, risen with and in Christ, breaking the bonds of all death forever.

Pentecost: The fiery light and waters of God's Holy Spirit, poured upon us, bringing forth fully the fruits and gifts within us.

Suggested Meditation

This drama and festival of the church year can begin within each of us now. In the sacrament of prayer, and in *each* sacrament of love in Jesus' name, we can witness the following (using *us* instead of *me* in a group meditation):

The risen, living Christ
Calls me by my name;
Comes to the loneliness within me;
Heals that which is wounded in me;
Comforts that which grieves in me;
Seeks for that which is lost within me;
Releases me from that which has dominion over me;
Cleanses me of that which does not belong to me;
Renews that which feels drained within me;
Awakens that which is asleep in me;
Names that which is formless within me;
Empowers that which is newborn within me;

47

Consecrates and guides that which is strong within me;
Restores me to this world which needs me;
Reaches out in endless love to others through me.

5

Discerning Our Powers, Fruits, and Gifts

As the living Christ awakens us, we begin to notice many changes within us and around us. Some changes will come swiftly, almost overnight. Some rise within us more slowly.

There may be changes in our health and our relationships to our bodies. We will probably begin to notice an alteration in our habits. We may begin dreaming in different ways. Perhaps we relate to other people, our communities, the world around us in a new way. We have changed attitudes towards our own selves. It is likely we move into a keener sensory awareness of sight, sound, touch, scent, taste. We are able to *feel* more deeply of joy, grief, love, anger, hilarity, hopefulness, sexuality, pleasure, intimacy, spontaneity, ecstasy. It is more than likely that we begin to see new power to make decisions, to choose priorities, to know when to lay hold and when to release.

These awakenings can be called our human *powers*. As they awaken, rise, and are healed and released by God, they can be compared to wings that stretch and fly, to great horses we learn to ride, to powerful music or color surrounding us. These rising human powers are not too strong for God. We need not fear that God will be jealous of them. God loves our full, unfolding *human-ness*. We are released to soar as high as we will, as fast as we desire, only with God's challenge and warning to let every power be healed, matured, guided in the deepening relationship of love within God.

Along with the awakening and intensifying of these basically human powers, we will grow into the experience of what the scriptures call the fruits of the Spirit. These are transformed relational qualities which rise spontaneously within us as living members of the living Body of Christ. In our fruitful growing, we experience deepening "love, joy, peace, patience, kindness, goodness, faithfulness, gentleness, self-control" (Gal. 5:22-23). As with the general powers, under God these do not awaken all at the same time or in the same intensity. Some of these fruits will appear swiftly in our lives as we bond ever more deeply with Christ. Others will seem to come forth more fully only when we have experienced a long time of inner healing.

It is significant that the fruits are not in any way opposite to our general human powers. Perhaps we could think of the fruits of the Spirit as the sanctification, the full baptism, of our powers within the communities of Christ in order to build up the bonds and body of love, compassion, and strength. And though they mature in different timing, nevertheless they are, at least to some extent, shared by *all* Christians who grow in Christ. Indeed, we may say they are the outward and visible signs that one belongs to Christ.

The *gifts* are different. For each of us, the gifts are the powers or fruits especially called forth, emphasized, intensified in our lives. They are the specific powers or fruits made central and highlighted within us for a special purpose.

Some of us have only a few. Some have many. Each of us apparently has a major area of giftedness, and it is, perhaps, the supreme challenge of our lives in God to discern what this major gift is within us. This will be discussed in special depth in chapter seven.

In the general discerning of our special gifts, it is important to distinguish between our skills and our gifts. I was greatly helped when Sandra Yarlott (soon-to-be pastor and former co-director of the Center for Women and Religion in Berkeley, California) explained the difference between one's skills and one's gifts. A skill, she says, is a deliberately developed ability which, though important, useful, and helpful, does not necessarily nurture and reenergize us. A gift is a deep, perhaps inborn quality (like an inner spring or fountain) which energizes and feeds us. She points out that when we work mainly out of our skills, we quickly get depleted and drained. If we try to work mainly from the center of our gifts, we are reenergized in the very work.

As she shared these extraordinarily enlightening thoughts, I suddenly remembered an experience over thirty years ago when I was a student pastor. The Board of Home Missions of my denomination asked me to go for a whole summer to a large western city. My assignment was to interview four hundred families in a newly built section of town to see if a new community church would be welcomed there. During the first week on the job, I felt a strange depression, fatigue, and unwillingness to begin my survey. I spent most of my spare time curled up on the sofa napping, eating cookies, and reading mysteries! I had to drag myself out of the apartment to start my community calling. I wasn't afraid that I couldn't do the job. I knew I could do it, and, in fact, I did it reasonably well. We did get a flourishing core group started that summer which developed into a fine church long after I had left the scene. Looking back, I realize now that assertive organizational work was a *skill* I had developed, but it was not a deep, inborn *gift*. It was not natural to me. It did not rise from my center. Yet it was work I had to do over a period of several months, and there was little opportunity to do work from my gifts. Therefore I felt both inertia and fatigue during the whole process.

How different it is when I teach! I can't get to my class

fast enough. I am filled with excited eagerness. When the class is over, I feel that comfortable, almost satisfied tiredness that one feels after hard, but fulfilling work that rises from one's center.

This is not to imply that our skills are unimportant. We all need our hard learned skills for everyday life and for many aspects of our jobs and professions. But if our main work and recreation is solely or mainly an exercise of learned skills, we will probably not feel very renewed or fulfilled.

What *are* our deepest, most vital gifts? At Christmas and birthdays we think a lot about gifts and spend much time trying to find the gifts for others that will bring them the most joy. What are the gifts God brings us? Reflecting on this question recently, I found myself thinking of the tradition of the gold, frankincense, and myrrh that the wise men brought the newborn Jesus.

According to the tradition, the gold was the symbol of sovereignty, authority, power, creative action, leadership.

The frankincense, from which we get the word *incense* (often used for fumigation, purifying the air), was the symbol of the priestly role, the intercessor, the connector between the divine and the human.

The myrrh, extracted from a shrub, was a healing, medicinal ointment symbolizing the power of healing, tenderness, and compassion for the wounded and broken in the world.

These three great gifts were given to Jesus by God, symbolized by the gifts of the wise men. We see in Jesus' unfolding life the *fullness* of empowered leadership, the empowered revealing of God to humans, the healing tenderness.

I thought this over and wondered if we, who are in relationship with Christ, have *also* been given at least a measure of these three major empowered gifts. But in our human lives, we will not see the three growing in full equal power. Most of us will find ourselves *mainly* in only one of these categories.

If we are of the "gold," we will probably find in ourselves the qualities of natural leadership, power to organize, to take initiative, to call forth enthusiasm from others. Here we find the creators, the artists, the builders, the planners, the leaders.

Those of the "frankincense" find themselves enabled in reflection, thinking, teaching, discerning, meditating. Here we find the teachers, the researchers, the lawyers, the counselors, the writers, the analyzers who perceive and make clear to others the mysteries around us. Those of the frankincense are bridge-builders for us all.

Those of the "myrrh" will find within themselves the gifts of healing and sensitive awareness of others. These natural healers and lovers will easily discern the needs, hopes, and gifts of others. Those gifted in this way will intuitively reach out to others with compassion and tenderness.

Though we find ourselves mainly centered in one area, it is fascinating to observe that as our healing and empowerment deepen, we become aware of the growing presence of the other major gifted areas within us. Sometimes these are referred to as our "shadow sides," not so much meaning our negative sides, but rather our sleeping, undeveloped gifts. For example, if you have seen and experienced yourself as a "myrrh" person of healing and intuitive tenderness, you may notice in time that the "gold" within you of assertive power and vital enthusiasm is increasingly surfacing.

We might ask ourselves: Are any of these three major areas of empowered giftedness totally missing from my life? Do I feel afraid of any of these gifts? Which one did I have the most as a child? Which one now? Have the others recently begun to come forth?

But how can we discover more specifically what are our actual gifts within these major areas? Here are some reflection questions which help us to focus on, to think about, what might be called our "hot areas," the signs pointing to the undiscovered life within, the deep gifted empowerments.

What was something I loved to do passionately as a child? As we remember ourselves engaged in that activity, let's also think about and try to feel again what areas of body, mind, emotion, and relationship were involved. What did this activity seem to evoke in us? We can ask ourselves: Is there anything I am doing now which involves so much of me, which makes me feel the same way? If not, why not? What has gone to sleep within me?

What situation keeps rising in my life: the same kind of problem, the same kind of person entering my life, the same kind of opportunity offered? Is God asking me a question?

Do I have a special dream that keeps coming back? Do the symbols in the dream ever change? What in my outer life causes the change? Dreams are often a way by which our deep, undiscovered self speaks to us.

Do I have a special fear? When did this fear enter my life? Did it seem to come after a long period of feeling powerless or out of control in some way?

What seems to trigger fatigue and depression? Am I living mainly from my skills? Am I ignoring the genuine gifts?

What seems to make me personally angry? As I look deeply at the causes of my anger, does it feel as if my special gifts were violated, misunderstood, or threatened in some way?

What activities really give me joy, fulfillment; re-energize me?

Do I have a special, deep, instinctive longing and love for certain places, things, people, colors, music? What is this instinctive attraction and love telling me about myself? What aspects within me are evoked, called forth?

Usually we love and long for what we already have, potentially, within us.

Where in my body do I feel the messages of new empowerment, inner gifts? Do I feel any bodily areas of tense muscular contraction, restlessness, excitement, as if there were pent-up energy or congested power there?

What do other people feel and say about my gifts? I have noticed that when we act mainly out of our skills, other people may be admiring, but are often uncomfortable with us. Is it because when we push ourselves, we are also (subconsciously) pushing others? When do we sense that other people feel the most relaxed, healed, or energized by us? This seems of major significance as we discern our major gifts.

As we listen to ourselves, hear what our bodies are telling us, recall our memories, observe our emotional responses, experience what renews our energies, watch how other people respond, we begin to understand and accept the beauty of our God-given gifts. As they rise in our lives, we feel not only gratitude, but also profound recognition. They are like beloved, but half-forgotten friends. It is like a homecoming to relate to them. We begin to feel the delight that God feels for our special gifts.

Suggested Meditation

Arise, shine; for your light has come, and the glory of the Lord has risen upon you.

—Isaiah 60:1

Relax your body, resting on God's presence and love in whatever way it comes closest to you. Move your attention slowly and lovingly through your body. Are there areas of numbness, tightness, congestion? Touch those areas with your own hands if you can comfortably do so. Picture Christ, the one who empowers, laying gentle hands upon those bodily areas, saying to you, "Awake, O sleeper, and arise from the dead, and Christ shall give you light" (Eph. 5:14).

Think now of aspects of your life which seem numb, gray, half alive, weak. Picture Christ, the one who awakens, coming into your daily work, to your home, in your relationships, in your recreation—wherever you feel unawakened, unalive, touching you lovingly and speaking to you: "Awake, O sleeper, and arise from the dead, and Christ shall give you light."

Go with Christ, who empowers and awakens, to that part of you which you sense still lies deeply asleep. You can picture that part of you as a sleeping child, a bare tree or shrub, or in some other way that is right for you. Picture Christ lovingly calling forth your deep, sleeping, gifted self. "Awake, O sleeper, and rise fom the dead, and Christ shall give you light."

In your inner picture, what seems to happen to this sleeping part of yourself? Don't force or contrive a picture; just observe what seems to happen.

Ask the Awakener (or the inner symbol of your newly wakened self) to give you a symbolic gift which will help you to understand something about your deep gifts.

When ready, bring your meditation to a gentle close.

Be observant in the next few days and weeks for changes in your dreams, signals from your body, significant memories surfacing, new challenges and new open doors in your life, and observations from others.

6

The Misuse and Abuse
Of Our Powers

A few years ago, a local newspaper in our area printed a long article of case studies of at least half a dozen well-known community leaders, many in the serving professions, whose powers and organizations had become corrupt. It was a grim experience to read this factual account of inspired leaders and respected community organizers, whose lives and work, begun in idealism, had culminated in fraud, manipulation, abuse, and disaster.

As a nation, we have not yet fully begun to encounter and understand the significance of those 900 dead bodies of men and women and children there in Guyana, lying in the midst of a corrupted and collapsed dream of building a perfect community.

But we don't need to look at corruption in high places or the nightmare of Guyana. We look at ourselves and realize that, though the inner release deepens and the gifted empowerment rises, we are not preserved from risk or made immune to error and abuse. We realize that the greater the gift revealed within us, the worse the disaster in and around us when that power is used manipulatively and destructively. And the closer we walk with God and reveal God in our lives, the more appalling and destructive it becomes when we start, usually without intention, misusing our giftedness.

Personally, I think it hopelessly inadequate to use the

word *sin* to cover this total problem of misuse and abuse. Sin is our freely chosen *consent* to what we know is loveless, manipulative, destructive. It is a choice or consent made in freedom, knowing we had alternatives.

But there is also the *wound* from which we so often act: the deep fractures and traumas of the spirit from which rises the unfree responses of crippling fear or chronic anger.

Further, there is the engulfment, the sense of powerlessness, in which we feel caught, trapped, in a destructive situation against our choice. We do not consent from our hearts, but we feel overwhelmed and out of control.

Then there is what Paul calls "party spirit" (Gal. 5:20), which can become a form of mob spirit, group control, a community mind-set or lifestyle or program of absolutism. In this situation, often our individual freedom, choice, and consent are swallowed up by a group goal or ideal. We are no longer aware of ourselves as individuals with a choice; and we are no longer aware of others except as means to our ends.

And, of course, there is moral sleep, ignorance, unawareness, in which we are simply not aware of the moral significance of what is happening around or within us.

I believe we can see examples of all these sources from which evil can rise by looking at the biblical account of Jesus' trial and death, known as the Passion Story.

With Pilate and Caiaphas, who sat in judgment upon Jesus, we see genuine sin, a consent to evil made in freedom. Both these powerful leaders knew that Jesus was an innocent man who did not deserve death (Luke 23:13-16; John 18:14). Clear sightedly, in full awareness, from motives of expediency, they gave consent.

But with Peter, who denied Jesus the night of his arrest, I think we are seeing the results of sudden overwhelming panic, not a clear, free decision. Peter loved Jesus. He had never intended to deny his friend. In fact, he had said earlier that no matter what happened he would never do this. But like so many of us, he either ignored or was unaware of deep levels of fear and woundedness within him. He overestimated his strength, and when the critical moment came there in the courtyard of the high priest, fear overwhelmed him, and Peter publicly denied the one he deeply loved. Since he did not intend this act, did not give free consent, I do not see his denial as sin, but rather the tragic result of some deep, unfree manifestation of an inner wound (Luke 22:54-62).

As we reflect on the women of Jerusalem weeping and walking with Jesus to the cross, don't we see those who feel overwhelmed, powerless, engulfed? They knew something unspeakably evil was happening. But though they hated it, though they did not consent to it, they felt powerless to do anything about it (Luke 23:27).

Do we see, perhaps, the fanatical absolutist in Judas? We do not really know, but many think that he had intended to maneuver Jesus into the position where he would use force to bring about his kingdom. Was Judas one who caught the vision of a universal realm of peace in which there would be no more poverty, no more injustice? Had he become so possessed by his vision that he was willing to use *any* means by which his ideal would become reality?

I believe we see the moral sleep, unawareness, in the Roman soldiers who crucified Jesus. They were ordinary men going about their jobs, "obeying orders." Some of the worst evil in the world has been perpetrated by those who felt they were only obeying orders, and who actually were not *aware* of the significance of what was happening. But Jesus saw that these were men who slept, whose eyes were not opened, who neither sensed nor felt nor understood what was really happening. And for them he prayed the poignant prayer from the cross, "Father, forgive them; for they know not what they do" (Luke 23:34).

We find within ourselves all these aspects from which

59

harmful decisions and acts arise. They are usually inter-twined, but they are not the same. We need not only forgiveness of sin, but also deep healing, awakening, and empowering from God as we encounter the misuse and abuse of our gifts and strengths. We need it con-tinually. And the stronger we grow and the more gifted we become, the more we need it. The ancient biblical traditions witness that even (maybe especially) the *angels* need it!

We are not told why misuse, abuse, and resulting evil is allowed to exist in God's universe. We wonder in anguish why God permits the human error and abuse and destructiveness we see or read about in the news, or that we observe too often in our own lives and the lives of others around us. *Why* are we allowed to sin and destroy? *Why* does God allow our wounds to become so deep and devastating? *Why* are we permitted to remain morally asleep and ignorant? *Why* is a community's destructive momentum allowed to overwhelm our personal freedom and decisions?

One of my students once shared her feeling that it isn't that God *allows* evil and suffering. "Rather," she said, "God *endures* it!"

It helps to know that God is not standing far off, de-tached, merely permitting and allowing unspeakable suffering. It helps to know that God is right there with us in the midst of the pain, bearing it with us. But we are still left with the question, Why must even God endure it? Why did such a state of things ever enter the universe at all if God is both loving and powerful?

There is no easy, simple answer possible. We can only wonder, guess, surmise. But there is a question which helps make things at least a little more clear: What would be the alternative? If God forcibly prevented all misuse and abuse, would there be any moral significance in the universe? Creation would be only a massive puppet show, a rigged election. When God first said, "Let there be . . ." in the supreme creative act, was there not *risk* inherent in that first word? Did not real risk have to be present as the price of God's deep honoring of the choices and growth of all created beings?

Many years ago I read a science fiction story which still haunts me. I can't remember the title or the author, but I remember it was a story of a future age in which a great scientist, maddened by the evil and suffering in the world, invented a race of benevolent robots. It was their task to serve all human beings, keeping them from all harm and preventing all mistakes. They were infinitely kind, attentive, helpful. Nothing escaped their watchful attention. Eventually, no human being was allowed to do anything potentially harmful or dangerous. No one could drive a car, work with machines of any sort, fly planes, sail ships, ride bicycles, cook at hot stoves, use tools, tame animals, eat or drink unhealthily, read distressing books or see distressing drama! If people cared about anything too much, they were gently, but firmly hospitalized. If they became upset or passionate, they underwent brain surgery to calm them down. About the only things human beings were allowed to do were to garden (though not with sharp tools), to take short walks (though not in the rain or hot sun), to arrange flowers, to listen to bland music, to work with clay and soft plastics, and to converse lightly. Eventually the human spirit began to die. Even the inventor, now trying desperately to destroy his invention, was gently forced to receive brain treatment to relax him. The story ends here, with the vision of a benevolent, mechanical universe in which nothing—ever—is allowed to go wrong!

This is a nightmare vision indeed! This would be a universe without any moral significance or meaning whatsoever. With no real risk, with no wrong choices permitted, there would be no true humanity, no true sons and daughters of God. Without the choice *not* to love, is there any meaning to the word *love*?

What a radically different vision we are shown in Paul's powerful, poignant words in his letter to the Christians in Rome: "The creation itself will be set free from its bondage to decay and obtain the glorious liberty of the children of God. We know that the whole creation has been groaning in travail together until now; and not only the creation, but we ourselves, who have the first fruits of the Spirit" (Rom. 8:21-23).

God, who has renounced force over us, allows us to enter fully into the risks inherent in a meaningful universe. We, both the innocent and guilty, are allowed to experience the reality of the risk and the groaning. We have been allowed to experience the bondage and decay that rise from our wrong choices, both individual and communal. But these are as nothing compared to the bondage we would have experienced if God had not renounced coercion over us. "Glorious liberty," as Paul put it, is God's longing and intention for us. Continually, God, suffering with us, releases, awakens, heals, forgives, renews; but the risk must remain, or love and response would have no meaning.

One thing we definitely know. God has not deliberately sent tragedy and suffering upon us. Though they are allowed, endured by God, they are not God's *intention* for us. Not once in the gospels does Jesus say that God sends tragedy and pain either to test us or to punish us. Though the blocks that prevent full healing are many and mysterious, the New Testament makes it clear that God is *always* on the side of healing, release, and reconciliation.

We know another thing. We are given the witness in scripture that the day will come when the whole creation will freely accept this love, healing, and reconciliation. There will be no aspect of creation left weeping and alone. There will be no more desire to choose lovelessness. The risk and choice will be there forever, but that risk (that grave gift of God's honor) will be transcended by a creation joyfully and freely united with God in the embrace of lovers.

This is not a bland victory. God has paid a great price for love within freedom. At any moment, Jesus could have freed himself from the betrayal, arrest, trial, crucifixion. As he said in Gethsemane, he could have called upon the full angelic powers to save him (Matt. 26:53). He could have refused to enter Jerusalem when his disciples pointed out the great danger. He had already told them that he knew what lay ahead. He could have explained himself to Pilate. He could have fought with the sword as his disciples were ready to do. He could have joined the Zealots and established a political kingdom.

But with his consent to go through the worst that people could do to him, we see the true power of God, who not only renounces force, but enters into our pain. God pays the price, reaching into the very heart core of our resistance and hurt.

Whenever we hear of or experience some deep tragedy and are tempted to cry out: "Where was God?" we look at Jesus on the cross and know that God has always been right there in the suffering with us, weeping with us.

What does this mean for our everyday lives? It means that as we strike out and deceive in our fear and hurt, God turns and looks fully and tenderly at us, as Jesus looked at Peter. When we give consent to loveless destruction, God awaits, endures, watches in silence, as Jesus watched Pilate. When we feel overwhelmed, powerless, God honors our tears, as he did the women of Jerusalem. Where we have done harm out of ignorance and moral sleep, God forgives our unawareness, as Jesus forgave the Roman soldiers.

But this does not mean that God's love is helplessness. On the contrary! As Jesus said, "The yeast kneaded deeply into the very substance of the dough awakens and changes and leavens the whole loaf" (Matt. 13:33, AP). We are not left with only the suffering, bleeding, dying

Jesus, but with Jesus Christ, risen in the power of new, radiant life, offering us that newness.

In an old Easter hymn, "Jesus Christ, My Sure Defense," there is this verse:

> Jesus, my redeemer lives;
> I, too, unto life shall waken.
> He will bring me where he is;
> Shall my courage, then, be shaken?
> Shall I fear, or could the head
> Rise and leave his members dead?

In the very midst, the very act, of our misuse and abuse, we find the God who not only shares and suffers with and for us, but also the God who at that same moment offers the healing, forgiving, awakening, empowerment of resurrection.

Suggested Meditation

Give thanks for the close presence of God. And in that merciful presence, reflect on your recent mistakes, wrong choices, loveless or destructive acts.

Try to discern which rose from the anger or fear of deep inner woundedness. Ask Christ, the one who heals, to embrace and heal those memories and experiences which hurt you.

Try to discern which of these choices were made in freedom and with intention, knowing they were hurtful. Ask Christ, the one who forgives, to help you receive the forgiveness and repent, which means "turn around."

Discern where you chose out of a sense of powerlessness, helplessness. Ask Christ, the one who empowers, to heal and make radiant the center of your personal being, where God's own image, God's own light is to be found. Ask the Healer to repair the healthy boundaries, so that henceforth no outer force or alien energy may assault or violate your integrity of decision.

Reflect on those harmful choices made out of "party spirit," in which you had lost the awareness of persons as you worked for your ideal, goal, or program. Ask to be forgiven and released from the manipulative force by which you violated the freedom and value of others.

Ask Christ, the one who awakens, to show you that part of you which is morally sleeping, and reflect on the loveless choices and acts which rose from ignorance and unawareness. Ask to be strengthened and held by God in the deep shock and pain we feel as we are awakened to what we have done in ignorance and moral sleep. Remember that *Christ himself* prayed from the cross for us who wounded others, unaware of what we did. Enter into the reality and power of Jesus' prayer for us, as you waken in guilt and shock. I think he knew then, and knows now, what we would feel as we awoke to the tragedy of our moral sleep. But that prayer is there for us.

After these confessional reflections, read slowly and prayerfully, as if for the first time, God's response:

What then shall we say to this? If God is for us, who is against us? . . . It is God who justifies; who is to condemn? Is it Christ Jesus, who died, yes, who was raised from the dead, who is at the right hand of God, who indeed intercedes for us? Who shall separate us from the love of Christ? . . . We are more than conquerors through him who loved us. For I am sure that neither death, nor life, nor angels, nor principalities, nor things present, nor things to come, nor powers, nor height, nor depth, nor anything else in all creation, will be able to separate us from the love of God in Christ Jesus our Lord.

—Romans 8:31-39

7

Discovering and Healing Our Great, Central Gift

There is a certain dream that is shared by an extraordinary number of people. Whenever I speak of it in a class or retreat, most of the group members begin to laugh, nod, and share variations on its major theme.

In this dream, it is near the end of the school or college semester or work period. Suddenly, with an appalled sense of shock, we remember that at the beginning of the semester or work period we had registered for a course or committed ourselves to a project. And then we forgot all about it! Now it is almost the time of reckoning, and we realize that we have not gone to any class session or done any of the required work. Along with the panic and shock, we feel a loss. It had been an important commitment, and we had forgotten it!

Is this just an ordinary dream of guilt over a deadline? Considering its widespread persistence and vivid power, I think it is a dream that points to a very deep level within us: our major purpose in life, our unique gift to the world which we were born to share but which most of us have either forgotten or have never even discerned.

But where do we look to discover it? How do we find the core source of our inner spring of gifted energy? "Look for the treasure in the unexpected place," say the old legends, fairy tales, and even scripture stories and parables. And where within us is the unexpected place?

It is exactly that aspect, that area within us which we have for years tried to throw out, to destroy: our major personality problem.

Each of us has a major problem, a core fault, block, or spoiler within. It has always made trouble for us, gotten in our way, tripped us up, blocked the health of our relationships, frustrated our fine new resolutions for our lives.

We have tried to uproot this problem, get rid of it, even kill it. Probably in our prayers we have asked God to kill it or at least remove it. I remember certain retreats or church camps in which it was suggested that we write our major problem on a piece of paper. Then, while the leader built a bonfire, we were asked to line up and march past the fire (perhaps singing a resolute hymn), throwing our paper into it. This was supposed to symbolize our destruction of our main inner fault. Perhaps we felt better for a few hours; but within a day or two, behold, our problem fault rose like a phoenix from the fire, all the more vigorous for its rest!

We have used willpower, we have used good resolutions, we have confessed, and we have prayed. But for most of us, the problem flourishes like a perennial healthy plant.

After many years of trying the usual ways suggested by spiritual leaders of holding down, ignoring, killing my besetting problem, I began to feel guided strongly to try something entirely different. I am not sure what first made me see that there was another way. Perhaps it was the guidance given by Jesus: "Make friends quickly with your accuser, while you are going with him to court . . ." (Matt. 5:25). Or, as the New King James Version puts it: "Agree with your adversary quickly, while you are on the way with him. . . ." Who *was* my main adversary or accuser? It was certainly the problem within who was always getting in my way.

What would happen if I began looking at and listening

to my core problem? What if it had something important to tell me? What would I learn about myself if for once, instead of shouting it down or turning my back on it, I asked it who it was and how it got that way? Could it *possibly* be pointing to a supreme strength as well as a deep wound?

Some extraordinary insights began to occur. I began to share this approach with others and observed the surprising changes in their lives. For example, I had several sharing sessions with a woman who told me she was what is called in some medical circles a "hot reactor" when experiencing stress.

"I've learned to calm down, breathe deeply, and think soothing thoughts," she told me. "I begin the morning this way and float serenely into the new day. Then, at the first criticism, the first sneeze, the first hint of a threatening possibility of risk, I become unglued inside—instantly! I wouldn't dare take my blood pressure at those times. I've learned to cover up my ungluedness with a calm smile, so no one 'out there' can possibly know how vulnerable I feel. Perhaps I'm a more hardened case than most people, and even God can't reach this nervous, frightened core within me. I've always been so ashamed of it. Surely Christians shouldn't feel this anxious so much of the time. But no matter how much I pray about it, God doesn't take away my tendency to anxiousness."

Had we talked several years earlier, I would have had nothing better to suggest than bigger and better anxiety control methods. But now I shared with her what had been happening to me recently. "How about listening, for a change, to what your deep anxiousness is telling you?" I asked. "How about letting it come forth, perhaps like a scared little child or in some other way that is helpful for you? Then listen to what it says and let Christ talk to it."

We sat together in meditation, in silence. Then she shared with me that her inner fear did seem to appear as a shy, nervous little girl, her hair hanging messily over her face. "Knowing I was with Christ the Healer, I felt safe to start listening to this little girl inside me. As she told me how she felt, I began to remember many unhealed incidents: scary experiences at doctors' offices; humiliating rejection in school; high expectations at home."

My friend and I talked together about the longing of God to comfort this frightened, shy little girl within, who had never felt quite comfortable with her life or with other people. This was not a process that could be hurried. But each time my friend went into this deep meditation of letting her frightened child be comforted by Christ the Healer, she felt a growing trust and the expression on the face of the child seemed to change.

But there was another very important step. My friend began to realize that her great fear was a powerful energy *in reverse*. What was this power when it was healed? Might it actually be her gift, inside out?

She began to ask herself—ask God—what sort of person it is who is able to become so vulnerable, so frightened. "Slowly it was shown me," she told me, "that it is the sort of person who is basically loving, tender, and discerning who is *capable* of becoming a frightened person. My own deep, central gift of empathizing with others is the very same quality that can overreact in fear."

The sun rose for her! No wonder God would not and could not take away her core problem. It was her inborn, God-given, lifelong gift of tenderness! Yes, it needed healing of its wounds. Yes, it needed comfort. It needed transformation from its present manifestation of fear into what it really was—her unique gift to the world.

Now that she has learned to look at, listen to, and embrace her inner adversary as the dark side of what was meant to be her radiant light, she no longer tries to destroy this part of herself. Instead, she asks Christ the Healer, the Renewer, to put healing arms around the fear when it shows up and to remind it that this is the self-same power that is capable of reaching with intuitive compassion into the hearts of others.

We are told in Psalm 118:22: "The stone which the builders rejected has become the chief cornerstone" (RSV, 1952 ed.). I have been told that the stones builders rejected in biblical times were usually picked up by the army to use in catapults. What a powerfully significant symbol! When we reject that part of ourselves which was meant to be our most radiant gift, our deepest energy, we do, indeed, use those parts of ourselves as instruments of destruction against ourselves and others. Perhaps there is no more dangerous weapon than our own deep, unhealed, uncomforted, unreleased inner gift. It won't go away; it can't. It was with us from our beginning. It stays with us forever, making life miserable for ourselves and others until it is healed and released as the power and beauty it was meant to be.

And the stronger that gift, the more devastating is its misuse. What would have happened to the world if Jesus had not given his gift to God's life and guidance there in the desert of temptation? What would have happened to the world if Adolf Hitler's inner, twisted, wounded, extraordinary power had been healed in time?

For most of us, this is not a quick, overnight healing and release. Because the gift is so deep and central, because for so long it has been wounded, because for so long we have been trained to ignore it, hate it, misuse it, all our lives we will be learning to deepen the encounter of healing. Fortunately, as soon as we recognize the actual existence of this core problem/gift, as soon as we are able to begin listening to it and allowing God to reach healing hands to its very center, the gift begins to show its true and beautiful nature. We will begin to see that the inner, gifted power of the angry person is that same energy which fuels the hunger and thirst for justice. We will begin to see that the very power in reverse which makes us overcontrolling is that same ability which, when healed, makes us powerful in strength and balanced discernment. Beneath the woundedness of over-control we often find profound, creative springs.

What is the true face of inertia, lack of self-discipline, lack of healthy boundaries? Deeper than the fault, deeper than the woundedness that gave rise to the fault, there is the integrity which caused that person, long ago, to put on the brakes against someone else's timing and lifestyle which had been projected onto him or her. When increasingly healed, the person whose block has been uncontrolled inertia will find the central power of peacefulness and the gift of affirming the timing, needs, and gifts of others.

Beneath the woundedness of greed and possessiveness, we find the radiant potentiality of the lovers of the world, who often are gifted with the powers to heal.

Beneath the woundedness that expresses itself with the anesthetic of addictions, we see the capacity for ecstasy, the keen sensitivity and capacity to feel deeply which is often the sign of the artist, the creator.

I am definitely *not* saying there is no evil. Most evil is manifested by our unhealed powers. I am not saying that we may not need professional help and guidance from others. We should seek and accept such help without shame, for we are communal beings and find our deepest human-ness in warm interaction with others. I am not saying that we do not need to learn ways of bringing the symptoms of our problem within bounds. What I am saying is that at the beginning and during the whole long process of healing, we are called by God to search for and love the living image of God at the very core of all our misused powers. The very power of the weight that holds us down is the same power of the wings that will carry us to our heights.

What a difference this makes in our attitudes towards others! As we begin to see the hurt that lies beneath the fault and the potential beautiful power under the hurt, our resentment toward others begins to undergo a miraculous change. It is not easy, but when I am trying to relate to someone who is critical and manipulative, I'm learning to ask myself: *What happened to the little boy or girl within this person to make him or her feel so threatened? What deep wound still lives within this person so that defense–attack is the only way to survive?*

Then I try to ask myself a deeper question: *If this person were healed, what would he or she be like? What strength and beautiful giftedness would shine forth?*

If I remember to ask myself these questions (and all too often I forget), I feel an inner relaxation and lowered defense towards the other. I may still disagree with this person. I may still have to resist and to set some limits. But now that I am aware that there is both great hurt and great giftedness under the hurt, my feelings undergo a powerful transformation. Often the other person seems aware of the change in me and changes *toward* me.

Last Christmas I was waiting in a long line to make my purchase. Only one overworked clerk was there to take care of about twenty of us. Everyone was getting restless, and I could tell the clerk, an older woman, was getting tense. Then the woman whose turn it was to make her purchase, looked thoughtfully at the clerk and said: "How hard this must be for you. But you must have a lot of strength and efficiency to take care of so many of us!" The clerk looked a bit startled, though she did not reply directly. But about five minutes later, she suddenly said loudly to all of us waiting in line: "I want you all to know I am proud of you for being so patient. I've never seen such customers!" The change that had come over her and all of us was extraordinary. Both her tiredness and her gift had been affirmed, and she was released to affirm *our* tiredness and *our* gift.

I remember well a time when I was healed of anger and defensiveness. I had arrived, hot and irritable, at a retreat center where I had been invited to be leader. The organizer had forgotten to send me directions for finding the center. I was lost for hours, getting angrier each moment. When finally I arrived, very late for the opening session, I was in no mood to lead others in loving prayer. I didn't *want* to pray! I wanted to snap off someone's head. Someone introduced me to one of the guests, the Reverend Alan Hunter, famous United Church of Christ minister and world-renowned spiritual leader, which was a bit like introducing an angry Timothy to Paul. I was so annoyed that I barely bothered to greet him. I still remember, after ten years, the mixture of affectionate compassion and twinkle of humor with which he gave me a quick hug and put a glass of cold lemonade in my hand. My anger melted like ice in the sun, which is unusual for me. I realize now that he saw the anxiety that lay under my anger and the worry that I had messed up this retreat. Under the anxiety, I think he also saw the energy and vision I felt about this retreat. It turned out to be a glorious experience for me. I have never forgotten it nor how much I learned and was given and how much I was enabled to give. I believe that through his prayerful perception I was released to give the leadership God wanted me to give.

How can we learn to encounter our central gifted energy and thus encounter and affirm it in others? The following meditation has two major aspects: the healing recognition of our major inner hurtful problem and the encounter with our empowered gift which underlies the problem.

If the suggested inner images and symbols are not right or comfortable for you, ask God to give you better symbolic images. Or, sense where in your body you feel the focus of the pain, the power, and the gift, and sense the healing light flowing to those bodily parts.

Suggested Meditation

Your sun shall no more go down,

nor your moon withdraw itself;
for the Lord will be your everlasting light,
and your days of mourning shall be ended.
—Isaiah 60:20

Relax your body with gentle, slow breathing, claiming God's enfolding love. Ask for Christ the Healer to be near you in a way you can sense or picture strongly. Trust whatever way or in whatever form God's love comes to you, even if unexpected. Rest in that presence, knowing you are in a safe place.

When ready, ask the Healer to bring forth tenderly that part of yourself of which you are the most ashamed, which you most dislike, have tried to hide or destroy. It may come forth as a hurting child, an animal, a shrub, or in some other way. Or, it may come as a feeling only. God looks at this part of you with tenderness. Infinite compassion flows around it. Encourage this deep part of you to tell its story, what woundedness has caused this fault, this problem. Your inner child may weep, show anger or fear. It may wish to remain silent or even to hide. Do not force yourself to embrace it or to reconcile with it at this time. But the Healer offers to embrace and comfort the inner self.

If it does not yet wish to be touched by the Healer, it is enough that the light enfolds it as it dwells in this safe place. Allow the trust to grow slowly.

Try to discern if a wound lies below the wound. Does apparent anger mask what is really fear? Does anxiety mask genuine anger? Does inertia disguise a deep, unhealed grieving?

Give time for comfort and healing to flow around your inner problem self. This may be enough for several meditation sessions, until you yourself feel compassion and a true desire to listen to what is happening within you.

When ready, ask your inner problem child to tell you what gift it brings with it. What great energy, power, beautiful, unique gift lies there? It may wish to show its

75

presence, its face, its power at once. Or, it may wish to give you a symbolic gift which hints at the underlying empowerment. It may not be ready to do even this; it may need more comfort and healing.

Picture Christ the Healer, the Awakener, embracing and filling your inner problem/power with radiant, transforming light.

When ready, conclude your meditation, knowing that the deep healing and release is at work within the very center of your being.

> If I say, "Let only darkness cover me,
>   and the light about me be night,"
> even the darkness is not dark to thee,
>   the night is as bright as the day;
>   for darkness is as light with thee.
>   —Psalm 139:11-12

If this form of meditation seems uncomfortable or threatening in any way, leave it and enter into some other form of prayer. Never push yourself or allow anyone else to push you into any form of meditation which does not seem right for you at this time.

If nothing seems to happen in the meditation, just relax and let Christ lovingly encounter that apparent "nothing". If there seems to be resistance or an inner closed door, picture the Healer lovingly touching that block or door. That block or door is the way your living pain expresses itself. It is the very presence of your woundedness. Never force it open. God does not use force. It is God's radical tenderness that will bring about the transformation. Remember that God's love has always been shining in your wounded center, even before you prayed about it. But by thus praying, we give our consent for the deep healing to intensify.

You may need to return to deep healing prayer many times. Each time it will seem different as the healing expands and intensifies and as the empowered gift is wakened and released.

8

Guidance of Our Powers Through Christ

The radio in my kitchen sometimes acts strangely. I will carefully tune to a special station I want to hear, and often, when I walk across the floor, suddenly another station will come on without the dial being touched.

Obviously there is some kind of interference with the radio signal, either inside or outside the house. But the point is, I find myself listening to a program I didn't expect and don't want!

Do we sometimes, thinking we are within God's guidance, suddenly realize that we have moved to another center all together and are tuned into some other wavelength that isn't right for us at all?

One of the surest safeguards of guidance is the recognition of the *manner* of God's presence. Few of us have visions or hear actual voices, and, even if we did, they would not necessarily be from God at all. But as we deepen our friendship and loving bondedness with God, we begin to *sense* that which is genuinely from God.

There are so many interferences within and around us, just as there apparently are around my kitchen radio. Some of these distractions come from the wounds within us that often masquerade as God. These inner messages usually sound judgmental, condemning, compulsive. How different they are from God's true Holy Spirit which brings comfort along with the true, clear discernment!

Sometimes it is our very ideals and high expectations (perhaps internalized from others) that try to imitate God's voice. A young woman recently shared with me the fatigue, the hurt, the self-doubt that rose from a family that was loving, but highly perfectionist.

"Nothing I ever did was quite good enough," she told me sadly. "They loved me, but I never felt they were really satisfied with me. There was always the feeling, sometimes expressed, sometimes implied: 'Try harder, dear. Make your best even better. Let's see how well you do *next* time!' And even when I had done my utmost best, when I got all A's, for example, they took *that* for granted and talked about the next task ahead, when I must prove myself again."

As I listened to her, I suddenly thought of that old saying about God's attitude towards us: "Easy to please, but hard to satisfy." I realized that that is a dangerous saying, a compulsive saying. I feel now that God is not only pleased, but also is *satisfied* with each step of healing, each loving act or response, just the way healthy parents are not only pleased, but also satisfied at each stage of a baby's development. When the baby smiles, or sits up for the first time, the healthy parent does not think: "Yes, I'm pleased, but I won't really rest content until I see her walking up to receive her graduation diploma."

Obviously the parent hopes and expects to see that baby grow up and graduate, but for now, that smile, that sitting up is perfect, is satisfactory—and completely so.

We are told in the great drama of Creation in Genesis that at each stage of the unfolding creative act and response, God called it good. God is not shown as saying: "Yes, that's all very well, but let's hurry on to the next step and do even better." We get the feeling that each stage, each step, was perfect in and of itself and that God fully celebrated it, delighted in it.

This is descriptive of a true love relationship, not a

performance. Isn't this what Jesus meant when he said, "You, therefore, must be perfect, as your heavenly Father is perfect" (Matt. 5:48). Read verses 43-47 in that chapter. Jesus is talking about love and the relationship of love. He is not talking about avoiding mistakes or the sort of relationship in which we compulsively perform for affirmation which is never fully given. He is talking about the love that God has in which each step, each person, is fully celebrated with delight. Learning to love in *this* way is the perfection to which God calls us.

I believe now that it is only in the context of this kind of love, which God gave and gives to each state of creation, that the next stage, the new gifts, are able to come forth.

Therefore, we must learn to beware of compulsiveness or nonaffirmation masquerading as God's voice and guidance.

But this does not mean that the voice of God is weak. That voice, at whose command light and creation sprang into existence and whose living word holds and sustains them in existence, is not a weak voice. It is the voice of such strength that it can afford to love, praise, affirm, celebrate—and to judge. To judge does not mean to condemn. It means to discern clearly, to identify, to designate. God's judgment is not the opposite of God's loving mercy. It is a major aspect of that compassionate love. It is the clear vision of love, which sees deeply and in entirety the fullness of that which is loved.

So the voice of God's guidance within is one of increasing clarity and vision, helping us to perceive what is wounded and needs healing; what is sleeping and needs awakening; what is trapped by alien influence and needs releasing. So we should distrust any voice of guidance which does not increase our clear inner knowledge of ourselves.

Likewise, the true voice of God comes not only with clear perception, but also with the offered empowerment to choose, to claim, to lay hold of and internalize what we need. God the Enabler always offers a way and the strength for that way. We are not left in helplessness, armed only with our willpower.

But perhaps above all, God's true voice within us respects and honors our freedom. If we feel pushed, forced, our freedom overridden, we can be very sure it is not God's Holy Spirit speaking to us.

The true sense of God's spirit, as opposed to other influences, is usually a slow, growing awareness within us which depends on the faithfulness and the depth of our intentional closeness to God. It takes a while to grow close enough to another person to begin to discern what is or is not of his or her spirit, his or her personality. But after a while of relationship, we know the voice on the telephone, we instinctively sense the presence of *this* person, we could even tell from a letter without a signature whether or not it was this person's letter. "That is not *like* John," we may say, not referring to the handwriting, but to the sense of personhood coming through the letter.

I think this is what Jesus meant when he reflected on the nature of the close bond between shepherd and sheep as symbolic of his relationship with those who love him.

> To him the gatekeeper opens; the sheep hear his voice, and he calls his own sheep by name and leads them out. . . . and the sheep follow him, for they know his voice. A stranger they will not follow, but they will flee from him, for they do not know the voice of strangers.
> —John 10:3-5

In his fascinating book *And Jesus Said*, William Barclay explains the ancient background of this saying:

> Each shepherd had a peculiar call which his flock recognized. They would answer the call of their own shepherd

and not of any other (John 10:3 and 5). H.V. Morton tells that he saw two flocks of sheep being put together into a communal fold in Bethlehem. He wondered how they would ever be sorted out when morning came, but it was very simple. The shepherds stood one on either side of the entry to the fold and each gave his own peculiar cry; and each sheep ran to its own shepherd. In the fold there was no door, only an open space by which the sheep went in and out. At night the shepherd lay across that open space so that no sheep could get out and no raider could get in except over his body. He was literally the door (John 10:9).

Those who have loved and have felt bonded to God through Christ for a fairly long time develop a deep sense of recognition and response when God is speaking to them. Also, they develop an instinctive uneasiness when something, no matter how worthy and holy it may appear, does not sound or *feel* like Christ's spirit.

This growing closeness, this daily deepening love, is the only true safeguard of our guidance in daily life. It is the best means of discernment between God's spirit and the interfering influences around us. But the following questions are given for meditative reflection as we try to make a decision about an act, a relationship, a commitment, an undertaking. We can ask ourselves these questions at the beginning of an undertaking or in the middle of it if we begin to wonder if we are in the right place.

Do I feel free and not forced or manipulated against my consent?

Do I feel a strong sense of authenticity? Does this really seem like the right time, the right place, and that I am the right person for this task or commitment?

Do I feel a genuine sense of joy and peacefulness along with the difficulty? If, over a long period of time, we feel only pain, discomfort, and increasing difficulty, this is usually a sign that something is wrong. It is moving to see how often Jesus used the word *joy* on the night before his crucifixion as he talked with his disciples at the Passover feast (John 13-17).

Do I feel fed, strengthened? Do I feel a sense of deep growing and learning in the midst of the task or problem?

Is there any kind of fruitfulness, creative change? If we are only aware of slammed doors, frustration, failure, or nothing happening over a period of time, we are probably not a holy martyr. Rather, we have probably wandered onto the wrong path.

The final question is based on that poignant story in the tenth chapter of Luke, in which Jesus visited the home of his friends Mary and Martha in Bethany. Martha was busy in the kitchen and rebuked Mary, who was sitting quietly, talking with Jesus. Jesus answered her: "One thing is needful. Mary has chosen the good portion, which shall not be taken away from her" (Luke 10:42).

I think this story is widely misunderstood. It is usually interpreted as saying that sitting still in quiet contemplation is holier than activity. This simplistically misses the point. There is nothing unworthy in cooking and serving. Jesus enjoyed food and sharing meals with others, as is made clear in many biblical stories. And, for all we know, Mary may have been a better cook than Martha! On several occasions, a shared meal *was* the needful thing: at the Last Supper; at the beach breakfast, told about in John 21.

I think the point is that on *this* particular occasion, the one thing needful was to sit quietly and share as friends. Jesus must have needed so often the opportunity to talk to understanding friends about his experiences—especially at this time, when he had "set his face to go to Jerusalem" (Luke 9:51), knowing what probably awaited him there. It was a time for unburdening the heart, not cooking and serving. And this was what Mary was trying to give him.

This guiding remark is of increasing help to me. In any

situation of deciding between alternatives, I find myself asking, "What is the one thing *needful*?" There are many things possible, many things important, many things good, many things helpful. But in every case there is usually one thing *needful* that stands out from the others. This does not necessarily mean putting one's self last. Sometimes the one thing needful will be the need to rest, to allow ourselves to be nurtured, to re-create.

It can be asked on a momentary, day-by-day basis: on *this* day, the one needful thing is to visit a sick friend, to hold that friend's hand; on another day the needful thing may be to write my congressional representative about pollution or means by which to save the rain forests or ozone layer; on yet another day the needful thing may be to take my child to the zoo or go square dancing; and on still another, we know that God is awakening in our hearts the need to face and start healing an addiction or doing something about the homeless in our town.

Or, this question may be asked on a long-term basis when trying to decide who to marry or what sort of job or profession to choose. What person, what work, seems to stand head and shoulders above the others? What is the person or work so central to our hearts that it has become necessary to our lives?

"Follow your longing, and it will lead you to God," is an old and wise saying I have heard. This does not mean every passing wish or desire. It means the steady, deep longing within us which we must learn to recognize and to listen to. For at this point is usually to be found God's will for us.

Sometimes we do discern God's will for us through the deep longing, the sense of authenticity, but we are prevented from following that guidance. Perhaps we are prevented by poverty, illness, or lack of opportunity for the sort of work we would really like to do. Perhaps we are deeply involved with responsibilities to others whose needs hold us back. Perhaps we feel engulfed and do not see any way out to follow freely the sense of guidance. What then?

First, we must realize that God neither condemns us nor leaves us because we feel trapped. But we should be equally clear that God has not intended for us a life of such frustration and unfreedom. The God we see through Jesus longs passionately for our release to follow our longing.

When trapped or held down, while waiting and working for release, we can begin to practice freedom of creative choice in small ways, but in ways that make a difference.

When I was pastor for several years in one of this country's largest cities, I often felt overwhelmed by the massive poverty, the racial and social injustice, the grim, gray starkness of the city slums. How could anybody live in any sort of freedom, how could anyone discern and respond to God's longing, God's plan for their lives, when so engulfed by ugly surroundings and brutal social indifference? But as time went on and I learned to observe more closely, I saw that there were open doors, though small ones, everywhere. There were choices to be made between the loving act and the loveless act. There were the small storefront churches witnessing to a compassionate little community of concern. There were apartments in the great, dirty buildings where a family would put a pot of red geraniums in the window. Sometimes it seemed to me that those pots of red geraniums were God's own presence in those streets.

We read the accounts of those in concentration camps in which the choices were narrowed down to the decision to share a bit of bread and soup, to move over a few inches in the bunks so one's neighbor could have a little space to sleep, or to whisper encouraging words to the person standing nearby in the forced roll calls in the freezing dawns.

These may seem small choices in unspeakable living

conditions, but they are the open doors which God sets before us, minute by minute. I suspect, within God's heart, there is nothing small or unimportant in any choice of loving response.

This does not mean, of course, that we are to submit to trapped, unfree conditions if we can possibly be released from them. Nor does it mean we are to be indifferent or insensitive to the trapped conditions of others. Some time ago I talked at length with a secretary employed in the office of a charitable organization. It was an increasingly unhappy situation in which she felt both dominated and manipulated by the office manager. The circumstances were having a devastating effect on her health and spirits. She came to talk to me, as a concerned Christian friend. She wondered if she should consent to stay in that position. "After all," she said, "If I stay, I would have lots of chances to learn about humility and how to forgive!"

As we talked together, I reminded her that Jesus left his hometown, Nazareth. We are told in Luke's Gospel (Luke 4:14-30) how Jesus came back to Nazareth and shared with his friends his vision and task. But the townspeople turned against him, and a crowd tried to execute him then and there by attempting to throw him down a cliff. "But passing through the midst of them he went away" (Luke 4:30).

This was the first time (since his babyhood) that he was faced with death, as far as we know. But this was not the right time, the right place, or the right cross. The one thing needful at *that* time was to live to witness to the radical, transforming love of God in a way that the world would never forget. At that time he needed to stay alive. Three years later, something *else* was needful.

"Release yourself," I advised the young secretary. "Only rarely are we asked by God to stay in a destructive situation. We are to preserve ourselves in wholeness and to release ourselves from injustice and danger unless we

85

feel especially called to a particular cross. And then we will *know* it to be our cross by the strength, peace, and authenticity we feel."

A cross to which God calls us is the choice we make in freedom to reach out to lift a burden or share suffering with another. No one else can tell us what is our own special cross, and no one may give us a cross against our will. Our cross is not at all the same as the thorn in the flesh of which Paul speaks (2 Cor. 12:7-9). A thorn is some problem which comes against our will as part of our human condition. But a true cross is offered in freedom and includes something of God's passion of compassion.

Suggested Meditation

> Behold, I have set before you an open door, which no one is able to shut; I know that you have but little power, and yet you have kept my word and have not denied my name. . . . I am coming soon; hold fast what you have, so that no one may seize your crown.
>
> —Revelation 3:8, 10

Relax and sense the closeness and tenderness of God. Have you some special problem or question? Read these discerning questions slowly and reflect: *What is the one thing needful?*

Listen to what your body seems to be saying. Do you discern a resistance? Listen to it. Look and listen more deeply. Is there a longing deeper still?

Do you feel caught, trapped in any way? What seems to be imprisoning you from following this longing? Is there anything you can do to release yourself? If that does not seem possible at this time, what *is* the open door, even a little one, that God has given in this situation? What *are* the choices you can make in this situation?

Rest quietly, breathing in God's breath and presence. Ask for some inner symbol of guidance to be given you and wait quietly. An inner picture, an inner word, a memory, a new awareness will probably rise from a deep place. Accept with thanks what comes. Though it may nct be immediately understood, it will be seen in the near future to have deep significance for your perplexity.

When ready, bring your meditation to a quiet close.

9

The Pain
Of Our Empowerment

As we turn on the television news or open the newspaper, we find instantly before our eyes the earthquakes, plane wrecks, wars, riots, epidemics. We are made intimately conscious of the suffering of people whom we do not know in places we have never seen.

In this generation, as never before, we are bombarded with the pain of the world through every possible means of communication.

Even in our weather reports, we now can see the advancing storm fronts that threaten us many days before they arrive. In a similar way, by the powers of medical scans and photography, we see the evidence of disease in our bodies long before we experience the symptoms.

Likewise, with the deepening of all our gifts and powers, there comes new awarenesses, new ways of experiencing, new ways of celebrating, and new ways of knowing pain.

Have you noticed as you grow in love and discernment, you feel the pain of others in a way you had never dreamed possible?

Have you noticed as you've grown in power and responsibility, you are given ever more difficult decisions to make?

As your sensitivity and empathy deepen, haven't you

discerned, painfully, the inner anger and misunderstanding of others and seen with keen sorrow the hurtful choices of others?

As your strength grows firmer, haven't you experienced more often the pain of having to set limits, to say no as well as yes?

And haven't we all, as we've grown in depth and power, seen more painfully in our selves those inner wounds and unhealed memories, that walled-off grief, loneliness, anger, and fear, still alive and weeping within us?

To grow in God, to grow in love, is not only joy, ecstasy, and release, but also dimensions of sorrow we had not imagined.

We read the poignant description in the Gospel of Luke, of Jesus' entrance into the city of Jerusalem on that triumphant Palm Sunday. He was filled with the radiance of his healing powers, loved and celebrated by hundreds who came to greet him. But we are also told: "When he drew near and saw the city he wept over it" (Luke 19:41). Jesus saw not only the cheering, enthusiastic crowds, but also the misunderstandings, the potential betrayal, the wrong choices, the ominous future for Jerusalem. In his empowered perception Jesus could look deep into the heart of those around him and not only see, but also share the pain of the confusion, the anger and fear, the unhealed communal sorrow.

The compassion that Jesus felt was obviously quite different from superficial or passing feelings of sorrow or sympathy. Rather, it extended to the most vulnerable part of his being. It is related to the Hebrew word for compassion, *rachamim*, which refers to the womb of Yahweh . . . There, all the divine tenderness and gentleness lies hidden. There, God is father and mother, brother and sister, son and daughter. There, all feelings and emotions and passions are one in divine love. When Jesus was moved to compassion, the source of all life trembled, the ground of all love burst open, and the abyss of God's immense, inexhaustible, and unfathomable tenderness, revealed itself.[1]

As we learn of God and grow closer to God, we begin to share something of this pain of God. As a young pastor years ago in one of our great midwest cities, I was so overwhelmed with the pain and heartbreak all around me, I forgot I was not feeling and carrying this awareness alone. I did not realize that much of what I was feeling was God's feeling of sorrow through me. Many of those in the helping professions, as they grow in love and concern, begin to share the pain of God's own heart; and many, like me, try to carry that suffering alone. I thought I could bear the awareness alone with my own small, limited stores of love, energy, and commitment. I forgot, as so many do, the warning of Jesus that the experience of this cross can *only* be carried safely if we become like branches of a living vine. The increasing pain of empowered awareness will break us, burn us up, if we do not become deeply bonded to the vine, abiding every day in the living vine of God's presence, drinking in that strength, nurture, and renewal (John 15:1-6). I used to be troubled by verse six: "If a man does not abide in me, he is cast forth as a branch and withers; and the branches are gathered . . . and burned." It sounded so condemnatory; and indeed, those words have been misused and abused during some of the more hideous chapters of church history, in which force and punishment were used to drive people within the fold of Christendom. But just recently I realized that no one is being coerced or condemned here. This is the living God speaking through Jesus (God the Gardener, lovingly speaking through the Vine), speaking the simple fact to us, the living branches,

[1]McNeill, Donald P., Douglas A. Morrison, and Henri J. M. Nouwen, *Compassion: A Reflection on the Christian Life.* (New York: Doubleday, 1982), 16-17.

that we will wither, we will experience burnout, if we try to carry the pain of God without the living presence of God!

This almost happened to me in my ministry. For months, deeply immersing myself in the suffering of so many around me, I had almost given up personal prayer. It was in the middle of a funeral service I was leading one day that I suddenly realized I no longer really believed what I was preaching. This came as a great shock! I did not, of course, dump this realization on the congregation at that time of communal grieving. I went on with the service, and probably no one but God and myself realized what was happening within me. But in the days that followed, I went through a sobering assessment of the inner hunger, thirst, and loneliness which had developed in my ministry. It was not the loving little church community which had caused this. There were many in that congregation wiser than I, stronger in prayer than I, far more experienced in loving and suffering than I, who would have helped me if I had shared with them my struggles earlier. But I had not faced with honesty the fact that I had ignored my personal relationship with God for many months, and yet I was trying to minister to others within God's pain and compassion.

I had not let God serve me. I had not let my community serve me. It would have startled me to think that God longed to serve me. Surely, I, the minister, was the one who should be serving! I had forgotten that though Jesus knelt to wash the feet of his disciples (John 13:3-6), he had let his *own* feet be washed and anointed a few days earlier by Mary of Bethany (John 12:1-3). And he was grateful for this loving, intimate service.

I forget this so often. I think many of us do, whether we are in a helping profession of nursing, teaching, counseling, or ministering, or whether, as Christians in ordinary, everyday church, community, and family life, we are trying to remain fully alive through close, warm relationship with Christ and with one another.

How can we remind one another that each day, in every possible way, we are to gather our strength from Christ, the living Vine? One way that helps me is to picture the risen Healer going ahead of me into difficult, demanding situations, filling that place with warmth and healing light, embracing the other people who will be involved with me, and welcoming me with warm love when I get to that place.

When Jesus said, "When I go and prepare a place for you, I will come again and will take you to myself, that where I am you may be also" (John 14:3), he was speaking at that time about his closeness to his loved friends and his guidance for them even through and beyond the experience of his death. But I believe that Christ is also speaking those words of closeness and guidance to each of us who love him now. I believe that the living Christ not only prepares a place for us after our death transition, but also for our next experience in *this* life, if we are willing. And when I ask the living Christ to go ahead of me, to fill that counseling room, that classroom, that pulpit, that office, with the fullness of warmth and light before I get there, I can *feel* that strength and comfort awaiting me and enfolding me when I enter.

There will be work to do in that future place and time. There will be problems to be solved and perhaps pain to be experienced. But I will no longer experience the work, the decisions, or the pain alone. The living Chist will be there ahead of me, carrying the cross with me (indeed, carrying the heavier part), guiding and strengthening me.

I have learned also *not* to think of myself as an ambassador representing God, trying to "front" for God. Nor do I, any longer, think of myself as some kind of channel through which the healing powers stream from God to others. I have learned now to think of myself as a sharing member of the consenting community within God's healing embrace.

I used to picture myself as a bridge between God and those whom I was counseling, teaching, or helping. But now I have learned to envision God the Healer moving amongst us *all*, touching, blessing, healing, awakening. I may be the one in the group who is doing the talking or leading in some way, and very often I will feel strength, insight, some unexpected illustration or thought rising from a source much deeper than my own. But I now feel that the light is not coming through me any more than it is coming through all of us. Shepherds though we may be, we are *all* also sheep, needing and sharing in the life of the one Shepherd.

Why does one need to picture anything at all or to pray and prepare ahead of time? If we are not careful to explain what we mean by this kind of language, we can easily give the impression that God is just waiting for the right words before leaping out to do our bidding. Far from it! God's love and God's presence are *always* with us, around us, ahead of us. And we have known of many occasions when, without any preparation or prayer, we sensed God's immediate closeness and help.

But by such intentional consent and prayer, we seem to be able with more fullness to claim, lay hold of, internalize, and *experience* the power of that love already so limitlessly around us. I think it is because God longs for our intentional consent and consciously claimed closeness as sons and daughters of God. That is part of our freedom and empowered choice which God honors.

But often we do forget to pray or prepare with intentionality ahead of time. Often there will rise an unexpected need or emergency for which we've not been prepared. But it is never too late. We can, at that very moment of awareness, claim the real presence of God and the literal enfolding light and guidance forever offered to us.

If it is a situation which is causing us extreme stress, we will often be given bodily signals: sudden lowered energy, pressure in the head, cold hands, clenched jaw, burning eyes, or other similar signs from our best friends, our bodies. At these times I have learned to pray inwardly what I've called the "rope's end" prayer:

Living Christ, I'm in over my head. This situation is getting beyond me. Take over; take over all the way. Fill this room, this place, and all of us who are in it with your empowered presence. I give all of this to you. I thank you that you are here and that your light and love are enfolding us at this very moment. In your name, in your word, in your power. Amen.

The swift response we feel to this manner of prayer is one of life's miracles. Those who have prayed such a prayer of utter need and release know the immensity of loving power that instantly surrounds and embraces them. I suggest you pray an inner prayer like this (in your own words) in your next crisis or stress situation. You will know, without any doubt, that God is in that place. You will know you are held with strength, that the Holy Spirit, the Comforter, has taken you and that place in loving hands, that light of an indescribable reality enfolds you like a garment.

Suggested Meditation

The doors were shut, but Jesus came and stood among them, and said, "Peace be with you." Then he said to Thomas, "Put your finger here, and see my hands; and put out your hand, and place it in my side; do not be faithless, but believing." Thomas answered him, "My Lord and my God!" —John 20:26-28

Relax your body, breathing deeply but gently. Give thanks that God through the living Christ is with you in this place.

Envision the living Christ, kneeling before you, showing you the wounds of love, taking your hands, asking you in what ways you feel that your gifts of love are hurting you or draining you. Share with the Christ what you feel and experience.

If inner picturing is difficult for you, know that God is there and try to sense in your body where stress, fatigue, or inner suffering seems focused the most. Or, think of recent memories in which you have tried to love, tried to help and which are causing you hurt.

Envision or sense that the living Christ is placing healing hands on the areas in your life or body in which your very gifts and powers seem to be the source of your suffering.

Ask to be shown ways by which the suffering can become a source of light and strength, even as Jesus' wounds were signs of enlightenment and love to Thomas.

Ask to be shown ways by which you can be drawn into closer daily living with God, so that the living Christ is not just a memory or symbol, but a living, empowered reality in your life.

When ready, give thanks and bring your meditation to a close.

Prayer for a Future Experience

When I go and prepare a place for you, I will come again and take you to myself, that where I am you may be also.
—John 14:3

Relax, and breathe slowly and deeply the presence of God and the breath of God's life.

When ready, think of some demanding experience ahead of you. Envision the living Christ walking into that place, that room, filling it with a warm, glowing light so it becomes a place of comfort and healing. Envision yourself entering there, feeling the warmth and welcome. Picture others coming in, also feeling the sense of love enfolding them and the warm inner peace welcoming them. Rest in that light.

When ready, leave that future place, but let its entrance remain open so that its healing light may shine on your path as you walk back to the present moment.

Rest quietly in God's presence, giving thanks. When ready, bring your meditation to a gentle close.

10

Celebrating Our Empowered Gifts

A few years ago, I was leading a prayer and inner healing retreat in a large, active church. In the early afternoon, we retreat members were sitting in meditative silence in the chapel next to the church sanctuary. Suddenly, without warning, the doors of the chapel were thrown open, a deacon rushed down the aisle to the altar, grabbed a large candelabra in each hand, and started back up the aisle. Through the open door we could hear a burst of music, laughter, and loud happy voices shattering our silence.

"What in the world is going on?" I whispered rather angrily to the deacon as he hurried by. "Can't you see we are *praying* in here?"

"There's a wedding about to begin," he whispered back loudly. "We need candles," and he rushed out. Smiling, curious wedding guests peered in at us through the open door.

Irritated, I firmly shut the door after him, and then suddenly began to laugh. Our scripture reading for our meditation had been Jesus' parable of the wedding feast as the symbol of the love and radiant power of God's kingdom, inviting us to joyful relationship. And here was a real life event happening that very moment outside our chapel walls. A joyous wedding was flowering all around our silence, and we frowned in irritation when it suddenly burst upon us. How often God enacts these little parables in our lives!

As I walked back to my seat in the quietness I thought how often Jesus scandalized the dour, correct people around him by laughing, going to parties, sitting down to feast with all manner of disreputable people.

Once he said (rather sadly, I think): "It is like children sitting in the market places and calling to their playmates, 'We piped to you, and you did not dance; we wailed, and you did not mourn.' For John came neither eating nor drinking, and they say, 'He has a demon'; the Son of man came eating and drinking, and they say, 'Behold, a glutton and a drunkard, a friend of tax collectors and sinners!' " (Matt. 11:16-19).

It seems that God really does want us to be happy, to celebrate. I am told that one great saint of long ago said wonderingly after a vision of heaven: "There is great *laughter* in heaven!"

It is the Easter season as I write this chapter. As we sing and celebrate the Easter joy, we celebrate the supreme central fact of Jesus rising from the bonds of death. Within that central joy, we are also celebrating our own rising, by God's love, into newness—new life, new joy, new ways of loving, new gifts, new powerful relationships with God, ourselves, and others.

Repeatedly we are told throughout scripture that our powers are given to us not only for compassionate service, but also for joy and ecstasy. We are urged to celebrate with God, to exult with God, to feast with God, to dance with God, to be God's full partner in love:

> The Lord, your God, is in your midst,
>   a warrior who gives victory;
> he will rejoice over you with gladness,
>   he will renew you in his love;

he will exult over you with loud singing
as on a day of festival.
—Zephaniah 3:17-18

Jesus told stories of parties given to which invited guests did not come. He told a sad story of a beautiful wedding for which half the bridesmaids had not bothered to get enough lamp oil to light the bridal procession. He expressed sadness when he saw the gifted, rich young man turning away from the full possibilities of his gifts. He reflected on the frustration of farmers who know that much of their seed will fall on rocky ground or be eaten by birds and never come to harvest. He shared the sorrowful vision of branches of grapevines which become detached from the vine, wither, and die.

I wonder if this might possibly be the true meaning behind that strange story told in Mark 11:12-14, in which Jesus withdraws the energy from the fig tree which did not give figs. That story has puzzled me for many years. The Bible story makes it quite clear that it wasn't even the season for figs! But after my experience in the prayer retreat, I began to understand what it might mean.

Jesus had just entered Jerusalem the day before, that Palm Sunday, in the full power of his longing and love. A few days earlier he had raised Lazarus from the dead. He had fed and healed so many who were hungry and sick. He had given countless people new gifts, a new way of life. Was he not *inviting* the fig tree, *empowering* the fig tree to enter (as so many others had) into unexpected, unprecedented abundance?

Jesus was not petulantly demanding the fig tree to get with it, to try harder, to use more willpower, to get its act together, to hurry up, to rush supply to meet demand! Jesus was trying to give a gift. The fact that it was not the season for figs made this offered gift all the more marvelous.

It is significant that the offered gift would enable the fig tree to feed the hunger of others. All Jesus' gifts enable us not only to celebrate and rejoice, but also to meet and serve more fully the deep needs of others.

When he told the sad, funny story of the wedding party and the sleeping bridesmaids, he ended with the words, "Watch, therefore, for you know neither the day nor the hour" (Matt. 25:13). Surely that refers to the unexpected gift that God often brings into our lives. Look back at your own life. When you fell deeply in love, was it at a suitable, convenient time? Don't you usually get your best ideas, your inspirations, your deepest longing and insights and encounters at the most unexpected, un-planned moments? Doesn't your most spontaneous, ir-repressible laughter well up at the most inappropriate moments? Don't your truest tears come forth as a sur-prise?

Do we each have a fig tree within us? Does God's own self come to us unexpectedly, offering us a gift we had not dreamed of having: a new power to love, a new chance to experience beauty, an enabling gift to forgive, a longing to heal, a new risk to be taken in our growing, a new way of relating to and celebrating our bodies, a new way to deepen our relationship with another person?

I remember once I was given inwardly a wonderful, new idea for the formation of a group that would have helped and enlivened the church I was attending at that time. But the idea did not come at a convenient time for me. I meant to get around to sharing it with others, to doing something about it, but I kept postponing it, wait-ing till I had lots of free time. Slowly the sense of excite-ment, joy, and power ebbed away until the idea seemed to die within me, just as that fig tree withered and died so long ago.

It is important to know that though the energy of a beautiful possibility may leave us or be taken away, God's love is *never* taken away. God never withdraws love. But we are often aware of a sense of sadness, a missed joy, a dying of that particular light. Other joy, other light will be offered, but that particular joy and light are gone. Another tree may well have been planted in that spot and given figs, rejoicing God's heart and feeding the hungry. But that particular moment in history, that chance to celebrate with God had died.

As we reflect on the beloved story of the prodigal son, we realize that though the father and the boy may have a better relationship than ever before, and, though the welcome home feast was genuine and joyous and the son was restored to full relationship, still, something had been lost. A new way of rejoicing is given. But we will never know what might have been the first offered way of rejoicing.

When we do respond to God's offered gift, God's invitation to feast and celebrate and grow, I think God loves to praise us. We often speak of praising God; we seldom think that God praises *us*. But the Bible is full of God's longing to praise us and delight in us, beginning with God celebrating and rejoicing in each unfolding phase of creation. Is our response to God's longing and love for us something we can actually *give* to God, that will, in some mysterious way, immeasurably increase God's joy?

I believe that the ability to praise, to receive praise, to rejoice openly in others, in ourselves, in the world around us, is one of the greatest of growing empowerments. This growing power to praise, rejoice, and to receive praise means that something very defended, locked-up, unhealed within us is beginning to be released, awakened, and healed.

I remember the sense of surprised excitement I felt when one year one of my students in class, a dental hygienist, reflected that our mouths are a very vulnerable area, and therefore, it is one of the most rigidly defended by our locked jaws, our clenched teeth, and contracted tongues. Perhaps this area of our bodies needs special tenderness and healing. When we experience difficulty in opening our mouths in surrender to the work of the dentist, I think it is because we instinctively know that our mouths are very close to our brain, close to the hearing, speaking, tasting, and breathing centers. It is a bodily center of great power and, therefore, a bodily part we want to close and protect.

It is interesting to observe how our hands go almost instinctively to cover our mouths when we are startled, embarrassed, confused, unsure of ourselves, or even thinking deeply. Is this related in some way to our difficulty in expressing praise with wholehearted, warm delight?

We all can think of deeply wounded people, inwardly frightened people, who are using this great, powerful center, the mouth, as a catapult to criticize and attack others. In our unhealed, inner woundedness, we usually both defend our powerful centers *and* use them for attack, and the mouth is no exception.

But the warmth that releases our jaws, lips, and tongue from rigid contraction is the same healing warmth that radiates felt and expressed delight. This does not mean we have to be constantly talking and singing. Sometimes a shining, smiling silence radiates our praise even more than words. But note what happens when you deliberately relax your jaws and mouth in the presence of others. Do you find, as I do, that you can more easily express your love and praise? Do you find it is even possible to accept wholeheartedly the gift of loving praise from another?

Note what happens when you begin your prayer, your shared thoughts with God, by deliberate relaxation of your mouth and jaw. Do you notice, as I do, that you can express with greater fullness not only your real anger and grieving, but also your real gratitude and delight? Do you find, as I do, that laughter, weeping, and singing seem to flow forth with greater released power?

This chapter opened with my amused memory of that wedding celebration on which I so firmly slammed the door several years ago. That in itself was not a serious incident, but it was a reminder to me (and I shared this with the retreat group later) of how many times God had come into the midst of my somber thoughts, offering me a gift and a chance to celebrate with God. We are not *just* grieving children to be comforted. We are not *only* wounded men and women to be healed. We are not *solely* broken human beings to be made whole. We are also spouses of God, lovers of God, beloved sons and daughters of God, created for ecstasy.

I have just read the vision and promise of Jeremiah, of the renewed wedding feast, the gift of joy to the ruined city of Jerusalem:

> "Thus says the Lord: In this place of which you say, 'It is a waste' . . . and the streets of Jerusalem that are desolate . . . there shall be heard again the voice of mirth and the voice of gladness, the voice of the bridegroom and the voice of the bride, the voices of those who sing as they bring thank offerings to the house of the Lord."
>
> —Jeremiah 33:10-11

And is not the promise made to us in our own inner cities of healed desolation and new empowered giftedness?

Suggested Meditation

> He brought me to the banqueting house,
> and his banner over me was love.
> —Song of Solomon 2:4

O Lord, open thou my lips,
    and my mouth shall show forth thy praise.
                                    —Psalm 51:15

Because thy steadfast love is better than life,
    my lips will praise thee.
                                    —Psalm 63:3

My beloved speaks and says to me:
"Arise my love . . .
    and come away;
for lo, the winter is past,
    the rain is over and gone.
The flowers appear on the earth,
    the time of singing has come."
                            —Song of Solomon 2:10-12

Without having seen him you love him; though you do
not now see him you believe in him and rejoice with
unutterable and exalted joy.

                                    —1 Peter 1:8

Relax your body, resting quietly in whatever way God
seems the closest to you.

Let your attention move gently through your body.
Note any places of tension and contraction. Note if there
is special tension in your lips, mouth, or jaw. Sense or
picture God the Healer placing warm, healing hands on
that bodily part. Or, sense or picture warm light flowing
into that bodily area.

Think of something you love to do. Sense God's hap-
piness and delight in you as you release yourself into that
activity. Give yourself a few moments of celebration with
God. Think of something you recently have done well,
done with all your heart. Picture God speaking to you
with joy: *"Well done, beloved. I delight in you!"* Try to
receive God's praise with full warmth.

Ask God to help you become aware of some gift, idea,

or possibility that surprises you. Does it come in a symbolic form? Does it rise as an unexpected thought? Do you sense its presence as a bodily feeling? Ask God to show you ways by which you can welcome it into your life.

Turn your thoughts to your body again. Does there seem to be a bodily center where the power of praise and delight is located or focused? Do you sense this power of joy and praise to be located near your heart? in your mouth? in your throat? in your abdominal area? Ask God to lay healing hands on that area so that it may be comforted, opened, released. You may need to come back gently and repeatedly to the area where your power of warm praise may lie deeply defended. But each time, there will be more opening and release.

When ready, inwardly smile at God and conclude your meditation.

11

Healing Empowerment
In Our Relationships

On long, cross-country auto trips, my sisters and I
would often start a certain song which must have seemed
endless to our patient parents. It was a song of many
verses and hand gestures, beginning with a forest, then a
tree, then the branch of the tree, then the twig of the
branch, then the nest on the twig, the egg in the nest, the
bird in the egg, the wing on the bird, the feather on the
wing, the hair on the feather. I believe there were several
other phases of progression which I've forgotten, but I
remember the joyous chorus between each verse: "And
the green grass grew all around, all around!"

As I look back on this repetitive and continuous song, I
feel we were, in some childlike way, celebrating communal reality. I remember feeling a sense of security and
interconnectedness. Within the living embrace of the
green grass, there were all these different beings—trees,
branches, nests, birds—distinct from each other, yet
sheltering and sustaining each other.

We were really singing about ourselves, held and
given life in a sustaining community. A child's earliest
experience of, or lack of, an empowering, life-giving community either affirms or fractures the deepest foundations of trust. At this very point lies the most profound
empowerment or woundedness. If one has been hurt or
fractured in this communal foundation of trust, and if

there is no intervening, transforming, and healing communal experience later, there may begin in that person's life a vicious cycle of deepening hurt received and hurt given.

Everything I have shared in this book about our individual healing and empowerment has limitless implications for our communal selves. We are small communities within: our bodily and emotional selves, our gifts, our wounds, our memories, our powers, our conscious selves, and our deep subconscious. We relate to the people around us the way we relate to our inner selves. As we deepen our consent to the healing of our hurts and powers, recognizing, embracing, reconciling with our inner problems and powers, we become more real and whole to ourselves. Then we begin to be aware of other people as real, as real as ourselves.

At a recent retreat, one of the pastors pointed out something I had never thought of. She spoke of the story of the blind man healed by Jesus (Mark 8:23-25), whose healing deepened in stages. When he was first touched by Jesus, he could see, but not yet in depth. People looked like walking trees to him. Then Jesus laid healing hands on him again, and he could see fully those people around him as human.

I was so grateful to this pastor for sharing this biblical illustration of an almost universal experience. For most of us, our healed awareness of others comes slowly. While still in our inner prisons, our inner, wounded blindness, we are usually aware of others only as walking objects, real only insofar as they serve our needs. But as we slowly become healed and whole, we see and sense at last the reality of others.

This awareness does not solve all problems. If our honesty has grown with our healing, we begin to realize that the encounter with others in Christian love does not necessarily mean affection or personal liking. Rather, it means that we have learned to see the other as *real*, as

God's own beloved child, wounded, tempted, gifted even as ourselves.

We learn that Christian love does not necessarily mean being always present, intimate, and vulnerable to the other. Jesus was certainly neither intimate with nor vulnerable to the Pharisees. He listened to them, shared thoughts with them, disagreed with them, and expressed honest anger when he felt they had betrayed their own task of bringing men and women closer to God in everyday life. But his perception of the Pharisees as God's children was always the foundation of his relationship with them. Otherwise he would not have bothered to get angry. Some forms of anger are manipulative and destructive. But there is a cleansing, empowering anger in honest relationships that are based on respect for the other (and one's self) as God's own child.

If we do not acknowledge the shadow sides of our lives, both individual and communal, fully facing the anger, the difficulties, and the conflicts, our polarities turn into polarization, and hostility grows like a defensive wall between ourselves and others. Sometimes we find this has happened already without our realization. How do we decide then if we are being guided out of a situation that is becoming increasingly destructive?

It is a sorrowful truth that this is often one of the early discernments and decisions we have to make as our empowerment grows. Often, our new freedom, our strengthening identity, becomes a threat to others, and they wish to hold us back or to leave us. Often our wounds and problems are more acceptable to others than are our released powers and gifts. This can happen in a one-to-one relationship or in a wider community.

Recently a young man sadly told me his formerly close relationship with his brother was becoming threatened. As he became inwardly healed of many inner wounds and began to celebrate new, healthy ways of life, his brother felt left behind and became increasingly angry

111

and defensive. Their times together turned into sarcasm and quarrels.

"What went wrong?" my friend asked, bewildered. "I thought as I grew closer to God and became healed that others would love me more!"

Usually we are loved more, by many. But others will pull away or become hostile. I think the truth is that as we grow deeper and freer, other people feel more *strongly* about us. Sometimes we arouse hostility because our very presence reminds them of their own unfreedom. But also, we should not forget that frequently we ourselves *create* hostility by well-meaning, overenthusiastic attempts to bring another person to whatever way of thinking and acting has helped us.

I always regret it when I see at retreat gatherings the presence of an obviously bored or reluctant spouse or best friend, who has been firmly dragged to the gathering "for their own good." And we all know the temptation to pursue our friends, waving the perfect book under their noses that will solve all their problems. Usually those books are the last to be read by our friends.

But sometimes, even when coercive enthusiasm is avoided, a relationship will become restrictive and destructive as we grow. Then we have to make the painful decision whether to stay and work through the pain, hoping for a miracle, or to leave.

In chapters four and eight, when I shared thoughts on leaving addictive lifestyles and relationships and on discerning our true cross, I suggested that Jesus' sad, but realistic words in Matthew 18:8-9 about separation might be our guidance. I think the same is true when we are making a decision about when to leave a relationship or community which has become destructive to our deep inner life. It is better, Jesus said, to separate from your eye or hand, rather than allow that which was meant to give you light and life to destroy you. I suggested in those chapters that possibly he was thinking of the pain of having to leave Nazareth, his hometown, rather than let them kill him or imprison his spirit.

How can we tell when that time has come? I know of no other way than the test Jesus gives: "If your eye is sound, your whole body will be full of light; but if your eye is not sound, your whole body will be full of darkness. If then the light in you is darkness, how great is the darkness!" (Matt. 6:22-23).

The "eye" can refer either to our great gift within that has become an evil energy, or it can also mean a relationship that had formerly given us light but is now a source of darkness and growing despair.

We can ask ourselves: *Is there any sense of light, vitality, hopefulness? Do I sense any healthy center? Is there any recent creative change at all? Is my strength, my energy, my hope, my joy being drained away from me and the other person? In short, is our relationship, our communal body, filled with darkness?*

But this pain is not the whole story. Increasingly as we grow healed and whole, we discover to our awe and delight that the experience of Christian love often does include the gift of affection, intimacy, openness, mutual sharing, and shared vulnerability to a degree we had not dreamed possible. When this happens in a one-to-one relationship, it is already an unspeakable blessing. But when it happens in a whole community, the depth of healing and released giftedness is almost unbelievable.

"For where two or three are gathered in my name, there am I in the midst of them" (Matt. 18:20). Surely this does not mean those gathered in a formal organization called "Christian." The word *name*, in the biblical sense, means the vital presence or spirit of a person. To gather in the *name* of Christ, in that sense, means to gather in that living presence whose love releases, heals, and empowers. It is this sort of fellowship that the Church, the Body of Christ on earth, was meant to be. All who came within its radiant energy were meant to experience the same kind of release that those experienced who came to

Jesus in the flesh. This is what it was meant to be. This is what it actually is—sometimes.

But even if we have not yet experienced the healing power of this kind of community, we can begin, in the radiant vitality of that Presence and Name, to seek out others who are ready for the healing encounter.

When this happens, we enter into what may be called an intercessory relationship. This means much more than just the act of articulate prayer for another. Intercession means to go between. This does not imply separating, but linking. In a healthy physical body, the more each bodily part, each organ knows and can enact its own identity and task, the more it can connect with other bodily parts in the radiant links of mutual renewal and sustaining. A healthy body is in a constant state of intercession, one part with another.

The whole universe and all its aspects is in intercession, from the microcosmic level of atoms and molecules, to the macrocosmic stars and galaxies. Through this interwoven, ever-renewed linking and bonding of energy, we see the immeasurable love and power of God flowing to each part, tiny or vast, mediating, connecting, interceding.

Therefore, our intercession for others is experienced not only in formal prayer, but also in every hand held out in loving compassion, every embrace of celebration, every shared laughter and weeping, and each act of merciful justice and just mercy which we struggle to express. All of these are acts of intercession and part of the central heart of passionate compassion which is God.

There is no wasted prayer or act of intercession. We do not always see the results we had hoped or expected. There are many wounds and blocks in this vast, living, groaning, loving, suffering universe. But I believe that every honest prayer and every intercessory act works in some way, not only for the person for whom we intercede, but also for ourselves, also for the world around us.

I believe every time we pray and act, the universe is changed in some way from what it was before.

In this sense, prayer does not merely inspire us to act, prayer *is* an action, a deep energy released that God will use to make a difference.

As we deepen in intercessory relationship, we discover that the core of our bonding is the mystery of each human being. I read somewhere that the way we perceive another person outwardly compares to his or her ultimate depth and mystery in the same way a bottle of ocean water compares to the ocean itself.

A bottle of ocean water may hold the true chemical composition of the water. From observing it, we learn something of its nature. But when we think of the ocean itself, the unexplored mountains and canyons beneath the surface, the strange forms of life within its depths, the far-off shores of its boundaries, we realize the bottle of water has told us almost nothing of the ocean's full mystery. What we see and experience when we laugh, weep, pray, or work with another person is only a tiny part of the awesome mystery of his or her full being. What that person truly is in his or her mystery is known only to God.

As the honor and the awe grow between ourselves and others, we will be less likely to push or rush other persons, arrogantly assuming we know what is best for them. We begin to respect the timing of the other, the free choice of the other, the distinct identity of the other. Then our prayer for the other person will not become a diagnosis, a prescription, or a brainwashing from a distance, but a release of the other to God's full healing light. We are there as part of the consenting community through which God's healing love may be more focused and intensified in the other person's life. When Jesus healed Jairus' daughter of her deathlike sleep, he took with him into her room her parents and three of his disciples: Peter, James, and John. Apparently he wanted or needed

115

them there as part of the focusing, consenting community for her healing. In this way, as we are drawn as partners into God's healing power, our experience of healing community becomes immeasurably deeper.

Perhaps the greatest miracle of all in this intercessory fellowship of profound linking and bonding together is the affirming of each distinct identity within the fellowship.

When Paul describes the empowered fellowship within Christ, he uses the human body as an example:

> For the body does not consist of one member but of many. . . . If the whole body were an eye, where would be the hearing? If the whole body were an ear, where would be the sense of smell? . . . If all were a single organ, where would the body be? As it is, there are many parts, yet one body. . . . If one member suffers, all suffer together; if one member is honored, all rejoice together.
> —1 Corinthians 12:14, 17, 19, 20, 26

What are we shown here? Not a blob. Not a one-celled, one organ creature. This is not a dictatorship. This is not a cancerous fellowship in which one form of cell wants to invade and transform all bodily parts into its image. Here we see *differences*, honored differences, each part honored in its special identity, each part connected to and helping each other part in the dignity of loving unity.

We can look in the scriptures to an earlier prophetic vision:

> The wolf shall dwell with the lamb,
>   and the leopard shall lie down with the kid,
> and the calf and the lion and the fatling together,
>   and a little child shall lead them.
> The cow and the bear shall feed;
>   their young shall lie down together;
> . . . .
> They shall not hurt or destroy

in all my holy mountain;
for the earth shall be full of the knowledge of the Lord
    as the waters cover the sea.
                            —Isaiah 11:6-7, 9

In the holy mountain of God (which can mean our own inner community or the communities around us), we aren't shown just *one* animal or animals which are all like one another. We see every possible type of animal, all shapes, sizes, colors, habits—but not devouring one another and not afraid of one another. We see them living in distinct identity, yet in peaceful playfulness, resting and feeding together.

Surely this was God's vision and longing when God undertook the great risk and said: "Let there be. . . ." The polarities, the opposites, were formed; the identities of dark and light, stars and earth, water and land, sea creatures, mammals, humans. It is clear that God loves the polarities and identities created first in God's loving heart and then developed in myriad forms over millions of years.

If God's vision of the holy mountain is to be fulfilled in this tragic world, it must begin within ourselves. We ourselves are a community meant to be that holy mountain. As our own inner community learns to live at peace, this expanding, loving reconciliation flows into the relationships around us, into the communities of our families, our churches, our neighborhoods, our cities, our nations.

Simultaneously, the healing outer relationships flow back into us, deepening, healing, reconciling, enabling on more profound levels within. That which has been for so long the vicious cycle of mutual hostility given and received in a downward spiral of destruction becomes the *healed* cycle of our communal bodies and their empowered individual members.

I began this book with my memory of the exultant

117

power of the wild geese flying in formation. But a better vision is shared in the last book of the Bible, the Book of Revelation. In John's vision of God's supreme central love and power, we are shown all manner of strange beasts and beings near God's throne. We are shown twelve different gates to the holy city. We are shown the tree of life with its many healing fruits. We are told that the very foundations of the city's boundaries are each of a different crystal and color. In this magnificently symbolic way, we are shown that the empowerment of love will increase and deepen forever: the identities growing more distinct and empowered and the love which unites these identities growing ever more joyfully passionate.

But this vision is what the supreme marriage and the marriage feast, so celebrated by Jesus, is all about! This is the divine risk of love God undertook when God created, embraced, healed, espoused, and empowered us forever.

Suggested Meditation

They shall not hurt or destroy
  in all my holy mountain;
for the earth shall be full of the knowledge of the Lord
  as the waters cover the sea.

—Isaiah 11:9

Relax and let your body quietly and fully breathe, as if breathing in God's own breath of life.

When you feel a quietness and warmth, sense the presence of your bodily parts, each so different, yet so connected. Think of your bodily parts with gratitude and thankfulness as they work together in harmony. Picture or sense God's warm river of light flowing through your body, blessing, empowering, uniting.

When ready, sense your inner complexity and the different parts of yourself. You might encourage your gentle, nurturing self and your assertive, creative self to come forth in symbolic form. Picture them reconciling, embracing, gifting one another.

Think of some fellowship or some community of which you are a part. Reflect on its differing powers, gifts, problems, strengths, needs. Think of each member as a full child of God, beautiful in his or her difference of type and timing.

Ask God to show you ways by which the members of your fellowship may more fully affirm and gift one another.

Picture the globe of this earth with all its different continents, climates, mountains, seas, forests, animals, peoples. Sense or picture God's arms around the earth, holding it close in tenderness and healing. See a warm, healing light glowing in the center heart of the earth. Watch the light expand until the whole earth body is filled and radiant with that warm light.

Rest your body, quietly breathing in this light. When ready, conclude your meditation with thankfulness.

Is it true that each community has its own group soul? And does each community soul carry its special wounds, powers, and gifts even as its individual members do? I believe it does. When John wrote the inspired letters to the seven churches (Revelation 2–3), he spoke to the "angel" of each church. I have sometimes wondered if he meant the deep spirit, the identity of each church fellowship.

Within the intercessory fellowship of our families, churches, races, genders, cultures, and nations, can we not pray within our group soul, even as we do for ourselves as individuals? Cannot we, as communities, envision the risen Christ coming to our wounded group soul, healing it, raising it from sleep, empowering its slumbering gifts? Cannot we learn to witness *together*:

The risen, living Christ
Calls us by our name;
Comes to the loneliness within us;
Heals that which is wounded within us;
Comforts that which grieves within us;
Seeks for that which is lost within us;
Releases us from that which has dominion over us;
Cleanses us of that which does not belong to us;
Renews that which feels drained within us;
Awakens that which is asleep in us;
Names that which is still formless within us;
Empowers that which is newborn within us;
Consecrates and guides that which is strong within us;
Restores us to this world which needs us;
Reaches out in endless love to others through us.

Amen.

Appendix 1

Guidelines for Entering Depth Meditations and Prayer

As we enter into depth visualizing prayer and meditation, we experience God's love in new and powerful ways. Also, we encounter our own deep selves in new and unexpected ways. The following guidelines are offered as suggestions so that depth prayer may be experienced in positive, creative ways, whether you are alone or in a group situation.

It is wise and helpful to begin the meditation by focusing on the loving nurture of God who surrounds and embraces you. You might begin with scripture reading, singing or listening to music, thinking about Jesus or looking at a picture of him. In this way, your meditation is put under the protection of God through Christ who longs for our deep healing.

Remind yourself that God understands your wounds, your hesitations, your fears, and does not demand instant complete trust and surrender. God is far more patient than we are and will not give up on you or leave you. Trust grows slowly. Take as much time as you need, and do not push yourself or allow anyone else to do so.

Remember that God honors your freedom. At any time

during a meditation, feel free to change the imagery and the symbolism. Feel free to close off inwardly the voice of the leader and move into some other form or prayer or meditation.

Be willing to move as slowly as you please through any meditation. Stop at any point you wish and focus on that moment.

If you are aware of growing discomfort or anxiety or you are experiencing more pain with any meditation than you wish to feel, feel free to leave the meditation. You are not "letting God down." God is not a torturer. You can pray in some other way. If you feel guided to do so, you can return later.

Remember that the love of God can come to us in many different symbolic ways: a feeling of love and comfort; an inner picture of Jesus; a sense of light; the feeling of strength holding you; a warmth within or around your body; an inner, spoken word; a strong feeling of authentic guidance or moral decision. Be flexible, and let God come to you in the way that is right for *you*, whatever others may be experiencing.

If you don't feel any special sense of presence or any strong inner symbols, be assured that God is near you always. God's closeness to us and love for us does not depend on inner symbols or emotional or sensory awareness. Sometimes we need just to rest on the faith that God hears and is near. You are still healing and growing.

If you become aware of inner defenses, closed doors, walls, or blocks, do not try to break them down or tear them off. Never do inner violence to yourself in your spiritual growing or let anyone else do so to you. These inner defenses have kept us strong during the years of our vulnerable woundedness. Visualize the living Christ encountering your defenses with full transforming love. God understands that our walls and closed doors are really part of ourselves, part of our deep pain and fear, and God will heal them with tenderness.

If you are aware of inner self-condemnation, self-judgment, scorn, and contempt, know that this is not the voice of God, but rather the voice of your wounded self playing judge! Ask God to heal that part of you also.

You may find that you wish to weep quietly during the healing meditation. This is natural and a beautiful gift from God of self-release.

You may find that you wish to sleep briefly during the meditation. Do not assume (or let anyone else tell you) that this is an attempt to escape from God and the self-encounter because you sleep. It may be that God gently lays your surface consciousness to rest so that your deep self may be reached more deeply and tenderly.

If you feel restless and uncomfortable during depth meditation, it may be a signal that God calls you to prayer through bodily motion or walking.

Occasionally talk over your meditation experiences with a trusted group or a friend. Listen, and reflect on their responses. It is helpful and healthful to have persons with whom we share accountability during our spiritual growing.

Reflect on the "fruits of the Spirit" growing in your life. Over a period of time, do there seem to be any real changes resulting from your healing meditations? Is there more understanding and compassion for others? Is there more awareness of your own needs, limits, wounds, powers? Is there a sense of something moving and stretching within you? Are there any changes in your health, your relationships, your values and choices?

Let God call you *out* as well as *in*. We are continually growing, as we are with any vital relationship. Prayer methods that may have been releasing and helpful in the past may become prisons of your spirit if adhered to rigidly. Keep alert and attentive to inner guidance toward new forms of prayer and relating to God.

Appendix 2

Guidelines for Leading
Depth Prayer for Others

The minister, lay leader, or group facilitator who leads others in depth healing prayer has a responsibility to be aware of the needs of group members at all times. It is a time of great openness, vulnerability, and self-encounter for the group members. The following suggestions are made in a spirit of respect for the dignity, uniqueness, and freedom of each person participating and for the sovereignty of God, who is the true leader of any prayer group.

Give some thought to the physical setting of the meditation. Is there a warm atmosphere? Are the chairs reasonably comfortable, or are there rugs and pillows for lying on the floor so that group members can relax their bodies? Is there a source of fresh air? Reasonable quiet? Is there a center of beauty or light on which people can focus if they wish, such as a lighted candle, a flower, or a picture?

Allow plenty of time for the bond of trust to grow between you and the group members and among the group members before you guide them into depth healing prayer. In an ongoing prayer group, you may wish to meet several times before you go into depth. In a work-shop or retreat, allow for at least a couple of hours for the group to share thoughts and feelings with you and each other and to feel comfortable together before you move into depth meditation.

Spend some time at the beginning sharing thoughts and meditating on the love of God, perhaps using scripture readings and some hymn singing. It is important that group members feel that their depth meditation is under the guidance and protection of God's love. Discuss the alternative ways and symbols through which God's presence may be known.

Be sure that at all times you are using nonthreatening, nonjudgmental imagery.

Make it clear and explicit at the beginning of *each* meditation that members of the group are free at any time to leave the room if they wish, to change the imagery and symbolism for themselves, to withdraw quietly from the proposed meditation, to move into some other form of prayer, to go to sleep if they wish. Sleep is not necessarily an act of avoidance. It may be a God-given sleep so that deep parts of the self may be reached more compassionately.

Remind your group members that they are free to stop and focus for themselves at any point of the meditation. They do not have to "keep up" with the others or with your voice.

Reassure them that if they do not feel any special presence of God that God is still completely close to them. Reassure them that if they become aware of inner blocks or doors that seem closed, they need not do violence on themselves. God will gradually heal these walls and blocks.

Remind your group before a memory-healing meditation that if the memory is too painful at present to encounter, it is enough to ask the living Christ to walk into that memory of the past without forcing the group members to go there also.

126

Do not urge your group to surrender completely to God, to release everything, to make a leap of faith. Most people are still somewhat afraid of God, and most people have deep unfaced wounds. Trust grows slowly as healing gradually deepens. Assure your group members that small amounts of faith and trust are enough to begin with and that God understands and has compassion.

Move through your meditation very slowly. Allow times of silence between each group of suggested imagery.

At the close of a meditation, give some suggested "grounding" images. Suggest that the group members become aware of the room in which they sit and the loving presence of others around them before they open their eyes. Allow a few moments of silence, perhaps with stretching and gentle face massage before talking together.

Suggest some time for group sharing and reflection. Encourage the members to discuss their experiences if they wish, especially any discomfort they may have felt.

Never *require* members to share their thoughts and experiences. Some may wish to reflect in silence. Help them to feel perfectly comfortable about keeping silence if they prefer.

If anyone seems to feel wistful or left out because he or she did not have the same kinds of experiences the others did, reassure everyone that each person's experience is unique, that God encounters us all in different ways, and that it is the *fruits* of the meditation that count more than the symbolic experiences within meditation.

Listen carefully to all group reactions about the imagery used, the timing, and the length of the meditation. You are all sharing this together as an experience of healing and growth.

Be sure that you, the leader, also have a chance to experience the meditations as a group member occasionally, with someone else taking the role of leader.

PRAYER, STRESS AND OUR INNER WOUNDS

Flora Wuellner

Prayer, Stress and Our Inner Wounds reminds us that the passion to heal was central to Jesus' ministry. 'God's love longs to touch and heal our inner wounds.' writes Flora Wuellner. 'The first step ... is to look with honesty at our own pain and to begin to open the door to God's love.'

Hurts from the past, fears of the future and pressures in the present often threaten to knock us off balance. In this gentle, sensitive, Christ-centred book, we are shown ways of ensuring that we experience God's healing love in the middle of life's storms'.
Joyce Huggett

FLORA WUELLNER teaches at the Pacific School of Religion, Berkeley, California. She is also an ordained minister in the United Church of Christ and has been an ecumenical retreat leader for fifteen years.

0 86347 042 4